Voices
From France

Michel Azama

Koffi Kwahulé

José Pliya

Véronique Olmi

Timothée de Fombelle

Voices From France

Translated By

Linda Gaboriau · David Homel · Maureen LaBonté
Morwyn Brebner · Don Hannah

THE BANFF CENTRE
PRESS

National Library of Canada Cataloguing in Publication Data
    Voices from France/Michel Azama...[et al.];
    translated by Linda Gaboriau...[et al.].
    Translations into English of five contemporary French plays by Canadian
    translators during the Banff PlayRites Colony, held at the Banff Centre.
    ISBN 1-894773-25-X

    1. French drama—20th century—Translations into english.
2. French drama—21st century—Translations into English. I. Azama,
Michel II. Gaboriau, Linda
PQ1240.E5V64 2006   842'.91408   C2006-904192-X

Edited by Maureen LaBonté
Book and cover design by Warren Clark
Proofreading by Lesley Cameron
Printed and bound in Canada by Hignell Book Printing

The publication of this book has been made possible thanks to the
contribution of the French Embassy in Canada.

THE BANFF CENTRE
PRESS

Banff Centre Press
107 Tunnel Mountain Dr.
Box 1020
Banff, AB
T1L 1H5
www.banffcentre.ca/press

CONTENTS

A Word from
the French Ambassador to Canada
by Daniel Jouanneau

Depuis plusieurs années l'ambassade de France au Canada apporte son soutien à une fructueuse collaboration entre le Banff Centre et la Maison Antoine Vitez (France) dans le domaine de la traduction en anglais de pièces de théâtre contemporains français.

Les cinq pièces qui figurent dans ce recueil, toutes récemment présentées sur des scènes françaises, ont été traduites, en présence de leurs auteurs, dans le cadre du programme The Banff playRites Colony.

Je forme le vœu que cet ouvrage retienne l'attention de metteurs en scènes anglophones du Canada et d'autres pays et les incite à inscrire ces textes à leur répertoire, permettant ainsi au public international de découvrir et d'apprécier la vitalité et la diversité de la création théâtrale contemporaine d'expression française.

Daniel Jouanneau,
ambassadeur de France au Canada.

For several years now the French Embassy in Canada has lent its support to a rich collaboration between The Banff Centre and the Maison Antoine Vitez (France) dealing with the translation into English of French contemporary theatrical texts. This collection of plays is the culmination of this effort.

The five plays featured here, translated into English in collaboration with their authors for the *Banff playRites Colony* program, were recently performed in France.

It is my heartfelt wish that theatre companies in English-speaking areas of Canada and elsewhere will take note of this work and find in it the material for new productions to give a larger public access to the vital and diverse realm of contemporary French-language theatre.

Daniel Jouanneau,
French Ambassador to Canada.

Foreword

by John Murrell

If it requires exceptional courage and sensitivity to be any sort of literary translator, *and I for one believe it does,* then it requires courage amounting almost to folly, and sensitivity amounting almost to obsession, to take on the task of translating a play.

Every language has its own untranslatable music, and every real author has her or his unique, non-transferable approach to transcribing the music of his or her language. This is true in non-fiction, novels and stories, and most obviously in poetry. But theatre, among all other forms of literature, carries its own special blessing and curse, as the most particularized and personalized kind of poetry that exists: a poetry defined by its distinctive linguistic music, channelled through each playwright's instinctive way of dancing to that music, but also filtered through the brains and hearts and tongues of various characters who are not mere mouthpieces for the playwright, but rather, in the best theatre (such as we have in this book), living, breathing, hurting and joyous, contradictory human creatures in their own right.

What sort of danger-scorning adventurers would choose to journey into theatre translation? Five of the most adventurous are present for your consideration in the wildly diverse landscape of theatre which is this anthology. Two of them are richly gifted playwrights themselves, one is a distinguished novelist and essayist, and the other two are inspired and inspiring theatre thinkers and mentors, as well as superb *and* seasoned translators.

Without beauty to translate, of course, even the most inspired translator would be mute. The five French-language plays in this volume posses the awe- and thought-provoking, eccentric, and universal power which Linda Gaboriau delineates so eloquently in her Introduction. Any translator of genius and ambition might be tempted by any one of these plays.

As a playwright and sometime translator myself, though, I want to seize this moment to salute the audacity and perseverance of those artists who go where many other brilliant translators would fear to tread—into the steam and swirl and quiet and despair and exultation and traditionalism and radicalism of theatre, this most immediately lifelike, and therefore most immediately paradoxical, of all literary forms. Translators of plays must be paragons of humility and of pride, capturing with precise reverence the original playwright's text, while also transmuting into an entirely new language something which is speakable, playable, and effective as a blueprint for live performance. I will go one step further, and say that theatrical translators must possess all the skills and sensitivities of other fine translators, plus a theatre practitioner's hard-earned knowledge of what will work and what will not work when presented by live performers to a live audience. I commend the translators of plays. I revere them and I fear for them, at all times.

A final note: it is certainly not accidental that work of such strength and clarity as the five translations in this book happened at The Banff Centre. For the Aboriginal people of western Canada, the Banff valley has always been a place of meaningful solitude, meaningful collectivity, of dreams, of inspiration. Today, for the creators, thinkers, and dreamers who come to The Banff Centre, this evocative location continues to provide both a laboratory and a launching pad for thrilling new investigation and creation. The intense privacy and the intense artistic encounters that constantly happen here inspire work which is as vivid, uplifting and challenging as this valley's topographical splendour.

John Murrell
Banff
March 2006

Introduction

by Linda Gaboriau

What do these five playwrights from Saintes-Maries-de-la-Mer, Paris (via Abidjan), Arles, Martinique (via Cotonou via Paris) and Paris (via the Vendée) have in common? One might be tempted to theorize about shared themes or aesthetics, but there is a simpler answer to the question. They are all playwrights who came to the Canadian Rockies for the first time to participate in the France/Banff Translation Exchange at the Banff playRites Colony. They are all the authors of plays that captured the imagination of the France/Banff reading committee—plays the readers felt would introduce Canadian audiences to striking examples of contemporary playwriting from the French-speaking world beyond North America. This anthology is all the more interesting because the plays are singularly different from one another.

The France/Banff Translation Exchange began as part of the multidisciplinary France/Canada/Banff Project, established in 1999 and co-sponsored by The Banff Centre, Foreign Affairs Canada and the French Embassy in Ottawa. At the instigation of Keith Turnbull, then director of Theatre Arts at The Banff Centre, it was decided that the playRites Colony would be one of the Banff programs to host a French artist every year. The Colony's mandate is, of course, to nurture the development of English-language scripts by Canadian writers, with the support of dramaturges and a company of professional actors available to read the works in progress. Francophone playwrights from French Canada and Quebec and, more recently, from outside Canada, come to the Colony to work with their translators on the English translations of their work.

I had the great pleasure of participating in the first five years of the Translation Exchange. The plays included in this anthology were translated in Banff during those years, 2000–2004. I was invited to participate in the first exchange as the translator of Michel Azama's

play, *Zoo de nuit* (which became *Night Zoo* during those two
wonderful weeks in the Rockies). Over the following four years, I
was an eyewitness to the translation exchange from another point of
view. Having accepted the position as Associate Director at the
playRites Colony, I coordinated the translation projects and
accompanied the four other playwrights in this anthology and their
translators as translation dramaturge. It was fascinating to observe
the dialogue between the playwrights as they elucidated their often
instinctive choices, and the translators, then stalking *le mot juste*
that would communicate both the spoken and unspoken meanings.
As coordinator of the Translation Exchange, I also got to play
matchmaker—an interesting role since the success of a translation
relies heavily upon the choice of translator.

Michel Azama, a prominent and prolific playwright whose plays
have been translated into several languages, was the first French
writer to participate in the Colony in 2000. I knew I wanted to
translate *Zoo de nuit* as soon as I read it. Between sundown and
dawn, in a squat in the deserted industrialized zone of an unnamed
city, three desperate youths (two boys and a girl with an infant
child) confront a middle-aged man who has come looking for his
son, or any son to whom he can play father. The infant's life is at
stake as the characters confront each other in a staccato ballet of
rage and longing. It is the characters' pent-up anger and occasional
flights of fancy when they struggle to make sense of their situation
that drive the dialogue. Their words are like Rorschach images of
their hearts and souls. They defy the rules of conventional
punctuation. The rhythms of their speech reveal depths of both
chilling cynicism and disarming innocence. The need to capture this
subtext in the translation is the kind of challenge drama translators
love. With the help of Keith Turnbull, acting as translation
dramaturge, and the resident acting company, Michel Azama and I
reviewed the subtle choices that go into a translation, until we were
satisfied that *Night Zoo* captured the taut and unforgiving tone of
the original.

In 2001, the reading committee unanimously chose *La P'tite Souillure (Baby Stain)* by Koffi Kwahulé. This play is a "family drama" like no other. The stranger who shows up for dinner the night of an anniversary celebration has come to settle a score of symbolic dimensions that the three members of the household refuse to recognize. As they project their respective fantasies onto the intruder, the rhythms and rituals of African masks and dances lurk in the well-groomed garden of this bourgeois couple whose only daughter longs to see their house, her prison, burn to the ground. Skeletons burst out of the closets when this avenging angel barges into their home and confronts their xenophobia and barely disguised racism.

P'tite Souillure required a translator who could navigate the waters of dark, absurdist humour and ride the wave of lyrical incantation that is part of Koffi Kwahulé's African birthright. Novelist, journalist and translator David Homel was the perfect choice. His lively translations of Haitian writer Dany LaFerrière's work, and his own trajectory as an expatriate American living in Québec, meant that David was no stranger to cultural references and how they inform a writer's themes and style. His bold translation of Koffi's play exudes the pleasure he had translating this, in his words, "orgiastic" drama in which biblical and mythical images collide with the petty hypocrisy of a repressed middle-class family.

The following year, the Colony hosted José Pliya who arrived in Banff from Martinique where he was, at the time, writer-in-residence at the Scène nationale de la Martinique in Fort-de-France. The members of the reading committee were all fascinated by José's play, *Le Complexe de Thénardier,* which explores a moment of truth between two women, The Mother and Vido, the servant in her household. Their confrontation takes place in an unidentified country in the throes of civil war. The horror of genocide fills the air. How can generosity or goodness prevail in a world where neighbours or next of kin will betray one another in their struggle to survive? The two women in this play have needed each other for very different reasons. Now, despite an obvious social hierarchy, suddenly the tables are turning. This complex situation defines the world in which The Mother and Vido face each other on this "last morning."

Although the canvas of *Le Complexe de Thénardier* is huge, the characters' emotions are painted in spare and poetic language. This is theatre in which Paul Claudel meets Jean Genet. It was clear that we needed a translator who would recognize the rich strands of theatrical tradition woven into this script. Maureen LaBonté was the obvious choice. Her translation, entitled *The Last Morning,* is subtle and precise. Her dialogue captures the innocence and transparency that guide Vido's appeal to her mistress, and the calculated cruelty and manipulation that drive The Mother's response. The characters' dilemma is a poignant illustration of the devastating influence a violent political context can have on the most intimate human relationships.

In 2003, the playRites Colony welcomed Véronique Olmi. Véronique travelled to join us from Arles in temperate Provence, only to arrive in the Rockies in the middle of a fluke May snowstorm that had all but closed the highway from the Calgary airport to Banff. She couldn't help but wonder, "What am I doing here in the Canadian wilds?" Fortunately, we had chosen Toronto playwright Morwyn Brebner to translate Véronique's provocative play entitled, in both languages, *Mathilde.* The dialogue between these two women playwrights was exacting and lucid, as they explored the subtle psychological shifts in Olmi's sophisticated *pas de deux.* The action takes place during one long evening when Mathilde returns home to confront her husband after an awful three-month absence. Pierre, the successful oncologist, refuses to believe that their life together has come to an end, despite the scandal of Mathilde's recent affair with a fourteen-year-old boy. Mathilde, the rather self-involved writer, admits that a child would have grounded their childless marriage, but she prefers to "lift off." Can her longing to be swept away by desire be compatible with the need for a deep relationship that provides the emotional security and creature comforts that allow a writer to write her books and a doctor to cure his patients? Mathilde and Pierre must take stock and resolve the question: "is this love?"

The last play in this volume is a haunting, minimalist piece by Timothée de Fombelle who participated in the 2004 edition of the Translation Exchange. One of the qualities of this script that seduced the reading committee was the incredible sense of place that Timothée has accomplished in this heartbreaking monologue entitled *Le Phare (The Lighthouse)*. A young man, referred to simply as "he," relates his last months on the island where his taciturn father was the lighthouse keeper. We, the readers, can hear the sound of the surf and the screech of the gulls, we can smell the salt air and the damp wool of his rugged sweater, and we can almost see the elusive horizon.

It was essential that the translator of *Le Phare* be able to recreate this sense of place. Playwright Don Hannah, who was born in the Maritimes and returns whenever he can, immediately came to mind. Knowing Don's own work, I also felt that he would be sensitive to this portrait of loneliness and extreme isolation. Don is not, however, a translator and despite his familiarity with Acadian French, he does not consider himself bilingual. Since we were convinced that Don was the right match for this project, we had to find a solution. The solution presented itself when Glen Nichols, literary translator and professor of literature at l'Université de Moncton, graciously accepted the task of producing a "literal" translation from which Don would develop his version. Don's version, *The Lighthouse*, recreates the maritime atmosphere of the play perfectly. And the rhythms in English capture the singular voice of this character who lives in his head and whose speech is as choppy as the waves that rattle the pebbles on the beach at the foot of the lighthouse. The version you will read is a powerful rendering of this tale of painful solitude, illuminated by hopeful and idealistic innocence.

Because "the play's the thing," I have resisted the temptation to
share anecdotes about memorable moments in which our visitors
from *la Francophonie* discovered the work of their Canadian
colleagues, and vice versa. The professional and personal exchanges
were many and stimulating. Participants will remember the evening
Véronique Olmi gave us a crash course in contemporary French
playwriting, from her vantage point as head of the reading
committee at the Théâtre du Rond-Point in Paris whose redefined
mandate is the production of new plays from the French-speaking
world. David Homel still remembers, wryly, his surprise in
discovering, when he and Koffi Kwahulé ventured off on their hikes,
that not all Africans are spontaneously close to nature. Koffi was
terrified that they would encounter one of Banff's infamous cougars
or bears. He proved to be much more at home when playing the
pinball machines in Paris where David visited him the following
year.

Several of us will long remember a moving conversation with
Michel Azama when he spoke of how he and Bernard-Marie Koltès,
whose all too brief but meteoric career marked French theatre in the
late eighties and nineties, had befriended Jean Genet in the last
years of his life spent in a squalid cold-water flat in the
Rochechouart neighbourhood of Paris. I haven't forgotten the
emotion in the room, the knot in Timothée de Fombelle's throat,
when he thanked Kevin MacDonald for his extraordinary reading of
Don Hannah's translation. There wasn't, as they say, a dry eye in the
room. Another memorable moment came when José Pliya told
colony participants about a trip back home to Benin during which
an incident involving his mother and the servant girls in her
household planted the seed of the play that became *The Last
Morning* in English. Moments like this in the magical cocoon of the
playRites Colony are all the more precious when shared by
colleagues whose "ordinary" lives are lived on opposite sides of the
Atlantic.

In closing, I'd like to mention that the France/Banff Translation Exchange is just that—an exchange. Our colleagues at Maison Antoine-Vitez, a remarkable organization devoted to developing fine French translations of drama from around the world, have in turn hosted Canadian playwrights in France. Between 1999 and 2004, Colleen Wagner, Marie Clements, Judith Thompson, Michael MacLennan and Kent Stetson travelled to France to participate in translation workshops focussed on the French translations of their plays which were subsequently showcased in staged readings in Pont-à-Mousson, Montpellier, Paris and Rouen. There would be many tales to tell of those journeys as well, but let's return to the matter at hand:—this first Canadian anthology of five recent plays from France presented in translations commissioned by the Banff playRites Colony. This volume provides Canadian theatre lovers with a unique opportunity to discover the thematic and stylistic scope of the theatre being applauded by French-speaking audiences around the world today.

                                                            Linda Gaboriau

NIGHT ZOO

(Zoo de nuit)

By Michel Azama

Translated by
Linda Gaboriau

Production Information:

Zoo de nuit premiered in March of 1997 at the Théâtre Varia in Brussels (Belgium). Philippe Sireuil directed. The members of the cast were Valérie Bauchau, Patrick Descamps, Philippe Jeusette and Alexandre Trochi.

Night Zoo was workshopped and read at the 2000 Banff playRites Colony. Keith Turnbull was translation dramaturge.

In 2002, **Night Zoo** was read as part of the National Arts Centre's inaugural <u>On the Verge</u> Reading Series in Ottawa. Keith Turnbull directed the reading which featured Matthew Fyfe (Jo), Gareth Potter (Miko), Alix Sideris (Sarah) and Todd Duckworth (The Man).

CHARACTERS

JO
SARAH
MIKO
THE MAN

─────────────

Nothing to specify about the setting, if not to say that theatre in my mind is a meditation on reality and not a more or less stylized reproduction of reality. The play begins at sundown and ends at dawn. M.A.

PART I

1

SARAH, JO.

SARAH
What did you do with it?

JO
The other guy's got it.

SARAH
The other guy? What other guy? How can you just leave it with someone else? With a stranger?

JO
A stranger because you don't know him, but I do.

SARAH
Since when? For an hour? A day? How long have you known him?

JO
Show me your tits. Pull up your sweater. Show them to me.

SARAH
If you want to see them, you have to give it back to me.

JO
Here. Take this.

He throws her a coin.

SARAH
It's worth twice that.

JO
You'll get the rest later.

SARAH
No.

JO
So just show me one.

SARAH
No.

JO
For half price.

SARAH
No. No credit on my breasts. How long have you known him?
For an hour?

A day? Longer?

JO
One for half price.

SARAH
Dumb shit.

Jo exits.

2

SARAH, MIKO, then JO

SARAH

You fucking shitty shit-eating fucker, what did you do?

MIKO

I forgot it over there. Or there.

SARAH

Forgot. Forgot? How can you forget how can you forget that?
Find it.

MIKO

Not far.

SARAH

Search hurry move find.

MIKO

Over there. Or there.

SARAH

You don't even know where you lost it.

MIKO

Not lost. Not lost. Lost no.

SARAH

You better find it fast or I'll split your head open I'll rip off your
balls with my teeth.

MIKO

Or maybe over there. Maybe.

SARAH

You don't even know! You don't have the vaguest idea! Search scrounge to the east scrounge to the west get a move on hurry move your ass run fly dance search dog search you little jerk search scrounge through all this shit that surrounds us faster faster faster than that!

MIKO

Don't yell. Don't yell. It makes me nervous sends electricity up my spine gives me prickles makes my fingers itch I can't help it I can't control it it makes me feel like strangling you. It makes me–

SARAH

Try let's see you try to strangle me.

MIKO

Or maybe it was farther down there. I can't remember. Help me instead of yelling instead of doing nothing but yell.

SARAH

I can't do anything. My stems have turned to rubber. My chest is caught in a wire mesh trapped like in an invisible block of cement even my heart has stopped pumping blood hurry up for godssake hurry the longer you wait the greater the risk of being too late.

MIKO

There's no risk. Can't go anywhere on its own.

dy is trembling trembling I can't stop it stop hands op trembling they won't obey me stupid bitches I feel like slapping them stop hands! Faster turd faster search find find!

MIKO

I search I go I run I sniff I crawl I fumble I dig I bend I take risks
I dance I run I slide it's slippery I stumble I fall flat on my face
but nothing poofff gone disappeared nothing nowhere I don't
know where I left it or somebody might've taken it maybe...

SARAH

Your blood never boils.

MIKO

No. Nothing. Nothing. I can't find a thing.

SARAH

Are all words so useless they can't bring you luck are my eyes
so cold they can't give you strength is your head so sick it can't
put you on the trail have you died before you turned twenty a
guy who can't even hurry for a woman who's going to die if he
doesn't find?

MIKO

You've struck out with me struck out everything goes wrong with
me I got no memory and I don't know how to hurry.

SARAH

You're the one who left it somewhere in this damn shithole
you're the one who better find it or I'll hang you I'll tear out your
eyes I'll stab you to death and fly you at half mast I feel like my
chest is going to explode.

MIKO

I can't find.

SARAH

Lap the ground search inhale through your snout let your tongue hang in the dust search with your feet they must know where they took you without thinking order them to go where they took you while your head was gone search with your guts with your fists and your rage with your sex did you piss somewhere did you take out your dick somewhere so it can remember too bathe in your sweat retrace the path of your sweat where did it start to run down your thighs grope the stone and the floor don't think don't reason don't bother let your ears burn dart your eyes that saw without looking chew the dust find the taste that got caught in your throat back there lick the ground so the foam runs from your mouth move climb into the recesses of your memory work scratch that thick skin row row cmon all the springs can't be broken in a twenty year old machine don't think demolish exhume feel scare yourself shitless be–

MIKO

Don't yell don't yell it sends electricity here.

SARAH

FIND!

MIKO

Up my spine.

SARAH

Don't stop for godssake spin turn look act don't stop!

MIKO

It gives me prickles in my hands.

,ine crank up the adrenaline my nails are digging so ,ds are bleeding.

MIKO
I can't help it I can't control it it makes me feel like strangling you.

He goes over and grabs hold of Sarah's neck.
Jo appears. Beat. Miko lets go of Sarah. Jo is holding a pile of blankets.

JO
I saw like this yellow spot moving in the desert of that
garbage heap.

SARAH (*to Miko*)
Garbage heap. You threw it in the garbage.

MIKO
I can't remember. Nothing no recollection blank memory I swear
a real black hole zero times zero I swear not on purpose just
forgot have to believe me.

Jo throws off the blankets. He's holding a baby in his arms.

SARAH (*to Jo*)
Give him to me.

JO
Tit for tat. You know what I want from you.

SARAH
That's not part of the bargain. That's mine nobody else's you can't
bargain with it.

JO
That's what I'm doing. If you want him back.

SARAH (*suddenly very tired*)
OK whatever you want everything you want now give him to me fast.

JO
If you promise.

MIKO (*to Jo*)
You can't do that.

SARAH (*absently*)
OK fine no problem I promise.

MIKO
That's enough Jo give it to her now go ahead. It's hers. He's joking he's gonna give it to you Sarah don't worry he'll give it to you right away he'll give it back he's just saying that to–

JO
Keep out of this, Miko.

SARAH
I promised he's a witness I promised give him back to me now don't make me–

JO
What do you promise? When you make a promise you promise exactly.

SARAH
I promise to take care of the old man.

from him whatever I ask you to in the way I told

MIKO
You can't Jo you can't do that to her.

SARAH (*mechanically*)
To extort from him whatever I Jo ask you to extort from him in the way I told you to.

JO
And this. (*He shows her the baby.*) This is my guarantee. My hostage. I'll keep him for now. I'll give him back when we've finished with the other guy.

MIKO
Don't do that Jo. I'm not on your side Jo if you do that your old buddy Miko won't be your buddy anymore ever Jo.

SARAH
You mangy pig you filthy mangy pig you lousy brain dead destroy sickie go screw goats in your leather gear you dumb fuck.

JO
Shut up bitch whore reject every dick in town recognizes you by your smell.

SARAH
Give him back to me. I promised. I'll keep my promise. When I make a promise I keep it.

MIKO
Give it back to her it's hers she made it nobody else can–

JO
Shut your trap Miko shut up this is between grownups don't get mixed up in this sweetheart. Today is a beautiful day. I woke up wrecked in the morning light but it's a beautiful day. Shut up.

Other people are a horrible drug you have to learn to do without.
If you're against me sweetheart you're against him this precious
innocent this cradle-dweller this little christmas package and you
babe if you can't shake your mind games and do what I say I'll
smash him to pieces I'll drop him from up here and you saw how
high it is how long someone falls when someone falls from so
high... And you know I'll do it if you force me to I'll drop the
little orphan off the ledge and a whole army couldn't prevent me
from doing it.

SARAH
    Never say that again Jo.

JO
    If you got the message no need to repeat it.

Baby screams.

SARAH
    He's hungry. It's not a thing Jo it's alive it needs a bit of warmth
    and milk at least.

JO
    I'm warm. He can wait for the rest. The sooner you carry out
    orders the sooner he can suck on your pretty bosom your pretty
    tits oozing sour milk.

SARAH
    You're pathetic Jo pathetic.

JO
        ~~ you love me.

                ly)

JO

And you expect me to believe you.

SARAH

I don't expect anything Jo only for you to lend him to me for five minutes because he's hungry. I'll give him back after and I'll do what I promised.

JO

No. This is my bond. Pay first and then I'll give your little Jesus back.

Baby screams.

SARAH

I hate you Jo I hate you.

JO

This time I believe you.

MIKO

And I hate you too Jo. I hate you I never would've thought you were capable of such a shitty thing.

JO

I believe you too sweetheart. You too.

3

JO, MIKO

JO

I sweat and I tremble when I touch you man. You attack me
baring your teeth. Your big rough hands tear at me with their
claws. You make me feel good Miko. I can swallow you whole
gobble you up put you inside me. I put you in my belly. I let you
punch me I protect my crotch you strike anywhere and anyway
boy and I love it you are my demon. Watch out she's powerful.
Don't take her for a walk in the moonlight Miko. Don't try to
possess her inside out she will possess you she's bigger than you
be careful don't get pushed around.

Miko has exited.
Jo exits taking the baby with him.
A man of 45 has entered behind their backs.

4

SARAH, THE MAN

THE MAN

We live in a world of brutes. Don't worry a deal can be struck settled or betrayed it's only a question of money or power. For the moment they have power over you but you and I have something they want to obtain don't we? Or rather I have this thing you have been ordered to obtain from me and that I'd be happy to give you if it is within my means of course.

SARAH

First tell me why you came here. You're looking for something and I want to know what. After I'll ask for what I'm supposed to obtain from you.

THE MAN

So ask me right away don't start with the impossible I won't tell you why I came here.

SARAH

How long are you here for?

THE MAN

Until I get what I came for. Shouldn't we stop making a mystery out of everything?

SARAH

You're the one who makes a mystery out of every sentence. First tell me what you're doing here.

THE MAN

Fine. If you have nothing to propose to me I'm leaving goodbye.

SARAH

Of course it's easy for you it's not your child. He's capable of killing that baby but you couldn't care less what do you care you have a whole world out there but this child is all I have nothing else period.

THE MAN

First of all, I have no pity for you secondly at your age you can still have lots of children. Thirdly I don't know what I'm supposed to do to help you since you still don't wish to tell me. Goodbye.

SARAH

Beneath your polished veneer you're as ruthless as the other two.

THE MAN

Propose your deal I'll tell you if I accept and if so in exchange for what.

The man exits. Sarah follows him.

5

JO, MIKO.

The baby is no longer there.

JO

You been to the sea?

MIKO

I've seen it. Once. It's blue.

JO

You're confusing it with postcards. You never saw the sea. Why are you lying?

MIKO

Fuck. If I had a comb.

JO

Leave your hair alone. It looks good like that. Dirty and knotted.

MIKO

Jo? Sometimes I think the world can't go on like this. It's really sick Jo. I say to myself if we were great we would've turned the world upside down we would've made it healthy again but we're still small.

JO

Right. We're all midgets.

MIKO

I think the god of happiness fell asleep a long time ago. Feels like he's been snoring since the beginning of this world and he's gonna go on snoring for a long time.

JO

> The world moves forward like a crayfish boy. A creature that walks backwards.

MIKO

> Look. A can of gas. There's some left. Help me find a tin.

JO

> A tin of what?

MIKO

> Any kind of tin. An empty tin idiot.

JO

> What are you gonna do?

MIKO

> Just wait. They'll see the flames from miles away.

JO

> You're crazy.

MIKO

> The whole landscape like one big torch the scorched smell from here to the stars.

JO

> Lay off.

Jo grabs his lighter away from him.

MIKO

> How long can you stare at the sun without blinking?

JO

You'll end up blind little jerk.

MIKO

Talk to me.

JO

About what?

MIKO

About me.

JO

Your voice. Your smile. Your teeth. Your hands. Your lips. Your eyes. Your hair. Your fingers. Your belly.

MIKO

Don't touch me. It hurts when you're in that mood. Men really turn you on, don't they?

JO

You turn me on. Nobody else. If you just like one horse you don't like horses get it?

MIKO

One day this sailor picked me up I didn't do anything with him just a little nice and after he stuffed a wad of bills into my mouth. Another day this punk wanted to stick me with this fat ugly girl he said was his sister I didn't want to know about the sister. An hour later the punk takes his revenge in a deserted alleyway he sticks his fingers in my eyes robs me and runs off. Some sailors carried me in their arms to the hospital.
Another day after three whiskies I sucked on the barmaid's painted nails and drank her in with my eyes. She was smiling and didn't resist.

Another day I go home with this couple. They make love and I watch them then I join them.

JO

So many people have laid their filthy paws on you.

MIKO

Yeah. But nobody ever touched me. Except you Jo. You're nice Jo. But I still miss–

JO

Always wondering what it would sound like if the moon fell on the earth. Don't you like it here? Aren't the two of us together here?

MIKO

And you always feeling glad you have pleurisy cause you were afraid you had cancer... No Jo I don't like it here. We just don't have anywhere else to go that's all.

JO

You think about her don't you? She turns you on, doesn't she?

MIKO

Who?

JO

Hypocrite.

Jo flicks the lighter and sets the gas on fire. They fall silent. Jo exits.

PART II

6

THE MAN, MIKO

MIKO
What's wrong what's wrong with you?

THE MAN
Nothing. Nothing serious. A dizzy spell. I get them once in a while.

MIKO
It's your age. This is no place for old men.

THE MAN
Old. Yes. You must be right of course. Yes.

MIKO
I'm an antenna. I capture everything. I could feel that you were in rough shape.

THE MAN
Don't you ever smile?

MIKO
I bet you're going to ask me for something. I can feel that too.

THE MAN
Me a luxury bum and you a pathetic star.

MIKO
You didn't answer me.

THE MAN
There's a certain stupidity about you that could be mistaken for a kind of grace.

MIKO
And you are totally old totally out totally absolutely passé. Your shirt too.

THE MAN
Pardon me?

MIKO
I said your shirt. Keep the jacket it's an old geezer's jacket.

THE MAN (*taking off his shirt, possibly laughing*)
Like the end of a party in the middle of cold trash cans with no money left for a taxi.

MIKO (*whistling in admiration*)
Is this gold? These cufflinks?

THE MAN
Not at all. They're fake.

MIKO
Cool.

THE MAN
You know how to go through life. You say "cool" you say "totally" you say "that rocks." Expressive words. Almost passwords actually.

MIKO

You're more and more ancient. Totally out of bounds. Forty-year-olds can't understand nineteen-year-olds.

THE MAN

Forty-seven.

MIKO

So obviously.

THE MAN

Yes obviously. Not everybody can be a little hood decked out in leather and nails with hair of barbed wire.

MIKO

You talking about me? If you keep it up I'll knock you flat you won't know which end is up you'll be left alone in this desert abandoned even by God.

THE MAN

Need a drink not God.

MIKO

Starting again? Sit down. Don't move breathe it will pass. You've got stains on your jacket you drank like a fish.

THE MAN

You stand there skinny white cold smiling and aggressive with your biker's jacket your jeans a real little clone a replica an artefact.

MIKO

You're really too much. Good thing I can't understand half of what you're saying otherwise I'm sure I would've beat the shit out of you already. You're really not the type no way.

THE MAN

And you you're young that's clear. I can see by your peach skin that gets puffy after a sleepless night your lank hair your prophetic wrinkles. The nice thing about you is all that surface.

MIKO

What do you expect. You and me we're not on the same planet. I can see that just listening to you walk. I'm not asking you for nothing I'm only talking to you because you're here that's all not every day you get to talk to a fossil like you that's all what else could I expect from you you're too murky you ooze depression the monster downer you drag around turns me right off you're so out of it you were out of style in prehistoric times.

THE MAN

Let's make a deal the two of us.

MIKO

No deal what deal I don't want to know I've got nothing to sell nothing to buy except my body that I can rent to you for fifteen minutes I'm warning the price doubles or triples depending on the customer's age and sex for you it will be the max.

THE MAN

You're on the wrong track.

MIKO

You're too fancy to be normal. People don't come here all fancy like that. You got the look all wrong.

THE MAN

I needed to meet people like you.

MIKO

You a voyeur?

THE MAN
   No.

MIKO
   Exhibitionist?

THE MAN
   Not at all.

MIKO
   Masochist? You come here looking for action?

THE MAN
   You're way off.

MIKO
   You want to play humanitarian corridor? Missionary-commando?
   You write novels? Make movies? You looking for guinea pigs for
   some experiment? There's fuck all for you here.

THE MAN
   There's the people. I've come looking for someone.

MIKO
   You just told me you're not looking for action.

THE MAN
   There are other things.

MIKO
   Get off my back will you if it's not money if it's not sex it can
   only be some weird head trip some old man's hangup and I don't
   give a shit about old men's hangups we don't live in the same
   world you and me between you and me there's the Atlantic and
   bridging the Atlantic's too much trouble.

Miko exits. Sarah still huddling in a corner stands up.

7

THE MAN, SARAH

THE MAN

Wait. Don't leave. Listen to me. Let's try to discuss this. If only
for a minute.
There's no getting around it. Believe it or not I'm in a hurry too
and every second I spend here costs me thousands of dollars.
Money never stands still.

SARAH

I could care less.

THE MAN

I thought you were an intelligent girl.
Personally, I started out very young and very low and I changed
jobs as often as I wanted and then some. All my jobs are high-
pressure jobs the worse the pressure the harder I work. I've
worked with more than eleven different companies and lost sight
of thousands of co-workers. My life is a perpetual quest. It's the
process of discovery that drives me to seek new friends to replace
the ones who no longer meet the mark with whom I no longer
have anything in common–

SARAH

You're a scumbag so ordinary nothing to brag about.

THE MAN

Don't waste your time preaching to me. Preaching is always a
waste of time it's for people who have nothing better to do.
The value of time has always been my greatest obsession and
one of the secrets of my success: there's no chair in my office
for visitors.

SARAH

Go away. I'm tired.

THE MAN

We're all tired. Everything about us is tired our century wakes up tired every morning.

SARAH

I'd like to bury myself in dope poker bluff sleep douse my mother's old age with kerosene and set it on fire.

THE MAN

Really you might succeed in surprising me. Tell me frankly: what can I do for you?

SARAH

Nothing. Someone like you can't do anything for someone like me.

THE MAN

Don't be so insulting. I'm not like those people from my class who claim their hands are spotless and in reality they have no hands at all. Wimps ectoplasms rather than out and out bastards. Cowards who always have soap and a basin of water ready to wash their hands of their pitiful crimes.

SARAH

Too many words. You're no different from those people. You have nothing but words for a shield to hide your unhappiness. All this is getting us nowhere. You have too many things to lose and I have nothing but that child.

What's your trip I'd really like to know why you're coming on to me playing the kind soul who'll come to my child's rescue?

THE MAN

We've wasted a lot of time beating around the bush. The child has already missed one feeding and his little stomach must be writhing with pain.

SARAH

You're a fabulous bastard.

THE MAN

I'd like to remind you that I'm simply trying to help you by reminding you of your situation and of the ways of getting out of it. Furthermore what are you doing in this district that only attracts people who are looking for trouble?

SARAH

I'm not going to tell you my life story it's full of holes.

THE MAN

Don't wallow in inertia like a slug move fight. I already told you if there's anything I can do I'll do it.

The man exits.

8

SARAH, MIKO

SARAH

I'm not talking to you I don't talk to strangers and I don't know where Jo dug you up.

MIKO

You're talking to me now and I've known Jo for a long time.

SARAH

And how come we've never run into each other?

MIKO

Jo kept us in separate drawers.

SARAH

I'm not talking to you.

MIKO

You're talking to me now.

SARAH

It just slipped out.

MIKO

Great. Let's talk or not talk but let's say what we have to say to each other.

SARAH

I have nothing to say to you. I look at you like I look at this landscape. I couldn't care less.

MIKO

I like you.

SARAH

What's with this guy? I'm too kind and you're too dumb. Are you still there? I told you I'm not talking to you.

MIKO

Jo told me your name was Sarah and that he didn't want anything to do with you anymore.

SARAH

I know your type. By heart. Gluttons blowhards navel-gazing wimps already lascivious hateful and angelic of course. Do you ever wash? You don't smell too bad. What do they have to say those flies that buzz around in your head and prevent you from sleeping during your panic-filled nights? You keep busy doing nothing. Already exhausted before you were born before engaging the battle you don't even know what battle I'm talking about. Already cut off from everything. Nothing but a little mechanism to vent the overflow of your petty instincts.

MIKO

Why are you insulting me? You don't know who I am.

SARAH

You are the vacant space beside Jo and no one ever knows who'll come to fill it.

MIKO

Keep it up. Shit on me. I don't care I'm like that black guy who gets his stash of coke stolen in that movie and stays cool as a cadaver...
I don't know if you noticed I saw that you're a woman but don't make me lose my nerve because otherwise I'll never know what to say ever again.

SARAH

Find him for me and I'll listen to you.
Take a good look at the unknown animal hiding in my eyes
you'll see that I'm neither man nor woman you'll see me exactly
as I am: vegetating in the wreck of my body. One half ate the
other it's growing like a tumour.

MIKO

Right Sarah keep it up. Tomorrow is a pile of cold ashes where
the moronic kids we'll be stupid enough to have will dance on
our dead bodies. You should pass your philosophy on to your
brat. The best guarantee for despair. Why make it so hard Sarah
you can also think a bit about happiness.

SARAH

Don't say the word happiness please.
It's freezing out nobody dares open their mouth for fear they'll
end up on the outside looking in. I can feel forces from inside
the earth rising and I'm terrified–

MIKO

We're talking about you and me Sarah not about the world. I'm
scared shitless. Talking like this won't... Don't worry Sarah we'll
find him. And I see the beauty of your woman skin.

SARAH

You're just like the rest of them going up in flames without
shedding any light.
Once I saw a juggler in a local circus a beginner he couldn't
catch his three balls so he panicked and pulled out four or five
hoping to catch one or two but they all got away from him he
broke out in a cold sweat to the catcalls.

MIKO

I don't get your story.

SARAH

You want to juggle with Jo and me and two balls is more than you can handle. Can't you see they're both getting away from you?

Miko exits.

9

SARAH, JO then MIKO

Jo enters.

SARAH

I didn't find out anything new he's tough a man who's used to succeeding at everything I don't know what kind of battle you're waging against him Jo and it's none of my business but you'll have to keep renewing your ammunition because this guy is a real war pro a real winner like you've never met before. Now Jo since you gave your word give him back to me.

JO

Not so fast. He's safe and warm.

SARAH

I wish I'd never been born.

JO

Drop the sob story. Nobody tries that on me it's too boring and nobody tries that on me ever. I don't want any girls around here. Girls are not men. And they're certainly not boys. Girls have got more meat than us and you can flog it that's why they cling to you but once you start you can't stop.

SARAH

God didn't spoil you. Where's your intelligence what feature of your face might be hiding it?

JO

I'll give him back if you leave. We don't want you around here. Nobody's interested in you around here.

SARAH

In that case I'm not bothering anybody and I don't see why you're so eager to get rid of me. Maybe Miko's got something to say about it.

JO

No. Today's not the day he'll say it or tomorrow.

SARAH

You say one thing but a man says one thing and wants something else...

Miko enters.

MIKO

I looked for him everywhere Sarah.

JO

All traitors. Even you sweetheart grubby and unshaven in the approaching dawn...

Sarah exits.

10

JO, MIKO

JO

So my shadow what's wrong?

MIKO

My shadow is that what you say what you call me my shadow
I'm the one who refreshes your memory when you can't
remember a thing and I call you weird because it suits you
weird... I hope that you can at least remember where you put the
little bundle?

JO

Memory's gone to ratshit. Nothing left suddenly blank slate blank
page sometimes it's better that way. When I want to remember I
have to make an effort it's like a handful of snow it's there I can
see it but it's already beginning to melt it's so delicate water
nothing but water I think I've grasped something and there's
nothing left.

MIKO

But you've got me Jo your living memory beside you. I can
remember anything you want from your life since I've been part
of your life I've got the essential right here and you know Jo if I
want I can open up without you. I take off and I say three words
and you're dead Jo three of those words would probably interest
a lot of people.

JO

No threats don't get a big head don't make all this fuss for
nothing. What do you want?

MIKO

When you look at me like that you look rabid. You know Jo that
I carry you round on my shoulders like a sick animal rather than
abandoning you to the hyenas and coyotes who are prowling
around here who are just like you part of your pack but who'd
gladly tear you to pieces and eat you for breakfast no problem...
I'm the stronger one Jo. The meaning and the circumstances of
your beautiful disasters I know them from A to Z and I don't
have little spells where I lose it... Give him to her Jo. Lay off and
I'll help you with the old man even if I don't know what you
want from him.

JO

Fuck you! Listen to you chatter like her. She's the one you want.
You don't brush your teeth you stink but you haven't turned
twenty it's the first time you're still a virgin sweetheart when it
comes to girls.
Now you've got this babe a romantic bitch with a little down on
her legs who'd give you some just to save her whelp with a touch
of virginal white cotton to hide the naked woman underneath
and at last you'd discover the total mystery of the total pleasure
of a woman.
Well do it what's stopping you? Go ahead the two of you. But I
still have to keep this little joker up my sleeve. Don't worry I
won't be playing it with her she's just one of the cards in the
game it's the old man who's sitting across the table from me and
it's him I'm playing double or nothing with sweetheart.

MIKO

You're wrong Jo. Tomorrow you will have forgotten everything
and you'll need to remember to keep playing your game and
you'll be happy to have me tell you that I can remember for you.

JO

Sorry boy you're putting the babe between us so far there's never been anybody between me and my memory. You underestimate me my shadow and it's a pity a pity to sell me short in your esteem sweetheart.

MIKO

Give him to me and I'll give you a brand new leather wallet.

JO

Go die.

MIKO

And a tie pin look with a diamond we should be able to get a lot for this and a silk shirt and pure gold cufflinks.

JO

Little jerk.

MIKO

I have something for you.

JO

You don't have anything I want.

MIKO

Here take this a platinum watch but you should keep this one because you'll never get another one like it.

Jo takes the watch, examines it carefully, sets it on the ground and crushes it silently and slowly under the heel of his boot.

MIKO (*tears in his eyes*)

I went to a lot of trouble getting it Jo. It was a watch Jo real platinum not a plastic one a watch like you'll never see again Jo.

JO

Go ahead go kiss her french it up together in front of everyone
go kiss her.

MIKO

Drop the act. The naked truth Jo you're afraid of losing me
that's all.

JO

Do whatever you want with her snuggle up to her in an elevator
and between two floors tell her devouring the whites of her eyes:
"You don't love me" that always gets them make your little scene
you must know how it's up to you sweetheart tell her incredible
things in a beautiful foreign language tell her on the phone: "I
filled the tank on my bike if I come right over will you still play
hard to get?" go ahead list off your strong points throw yourself
at her let a spine of silence enter your back lie in the grass with
her be melded flesh in a whirlpool an undertow let her silkworm
skin melt in your hands let the sweat from her wet hair flow let
her collection of hands explore your thorax pin you to the
ground like a bug find your passwords in a low voice at the foot
of the bed until your skin turns blue from caresses celebrate the
rites of benediction offerings salvation knock yourselves out
from the heart all the way.

Jo exits. Sarah enters.

11

MIKO, SARAH

SARAH

Make noise talk to me don't stop talking.

MIKO

My parents used to move all the time. Every time the same new house the same garden a load of plowed topsoil without a single plant and every time the same new trees planted in a line to make a hedge.

SARAH

Go on.

MIKO

My father always refused to commit himself. Forbidden to join a club forbidden to become friends with the neighbours forbidden to consider the house a permanent definitive home. Real industrial gypsies.

SARAH

Go on.

MIKO

My mother got used to selling everything never getting attached to anything that's what she got used to not even to us kids. My God Sarah I've got a fucking thing for you don't take off and disappear between two blocks it would kill me.

SARAH

Don't stop don't stop talking.

MIKO

How many people can still describe the place where they were
born? What a flat-out speedway our lives are.
We could have expected them to age well like wine or computers
now that they know how to make stronger houses dams roads
satellites invent two hundred varieties of roses and what else?

SARAH

Stop stopping all the time I need.

MIKO

You can rent anything. Lawnmowers mink coats and famous
masterpieces. You can rent an adult cypress tree for an hour to
plant on your father's grave just for the burial.
I remember. They cut the rope and he fell to the ground. The kid
didn't squirm the kid was watching watching his hanging father's
blue face stick out its purple tongue like somebody making a bad
joke the kid didn't say a word make a move he must've been
eight or nine years old that kid was me.
You're not even listening to me.
If you're thinking about something tell me what you're
thinking about.

SARAH

Meanwhile that other one the sicko who's never going to give
him back and he's not even crying anymore he's not even cold
anymore he can't feel a thing anymore and you nice very nice so
nice you want to keep my mind occupied you want me to forget
you little jerk you say you've looked everywhere and you won't
find anything now but you didn't do everything you didn't smash
his head in so he'd spill the beans you didn't listen to him sleep
so he'd unleash the truth in his dreams you didn't get him drunk
so he'd collapse on you and the truth would trickle out of his
mouth. You didn't do fuck all just talk my ear off so my mind
would drain like an old sink. Your blah-blah-blah is driving me

crazy. I'll teach you that a woman doesn't need so many words a woman needs proof every day and the only proof is to find him fast. So move your ass c'mon move.

MIKO
My God Sarah you've lost me. There are so many voices in your voice to make it that beautiful. Sarah you kick the shit out of me so bad I'm losing my head.

Miko exits.

SARAH (*alone*)
When I was twelve I shot a bullet into my head. It's been travelling through my body ever since and it still hasn't exploded it's looking for its point of impact...

Sarah exits.

12

JO, THE MAN

Jo enters. He's holding a switchblade in his hand. Both jubilant and threatening.

JO

Whatshisname the asshole the Son of the Father he said eat one another it's crazy how it caught on took root the seed must've fallen everywhere cause those words were so great. Eat one another everyone heard it and promptly obeyed. Obviously he didn't go so far as to ask us to eat ourselves. We haven't stopped eating one another and sucking each other's blood ever since. Anyway why go without can you think of anything better or more fun?

THE MAN

What do you want from me? (*Jo passes the switchblade lightly over the palm of his hand. Drops of blood appear.*) Perfect instrument I suppose for severing your problems. Tell me what will you get out of killing me?

JO

Pleasure.

THE MAN

Of course.

JO (*sarcastically*)

Killing is evil.

THE MAN

That depends. For money everything is if not allowed at least justified. If you kill for absolutely nothing but pleasure then yes you might say it's evil.

JO

I love it. It gives me a hard-on.

THE MAN

Oh well that's... isn't it... One reason... But... rather insufficient...

JO

Yeah? From what point of view?

THE MAN

Stop making yourself bleed like that it's annoying it's disgusting.

JO

What? The sight of blood? The sight of blood disgusts you? There's nothing but walls where there should be sky buildings shout with all their neons the trees are grey and herds roam the streets robbing and killing. When God made the earth he made it a woman and they fornicated. His seed is made of fire and blood and together they gave birth to nothing but monsters.

THE MAN

You're a poet.

JO

No I'm crazy.

THE MAN

It's better than being ordinary.

JO

Go ahead flatter me. I'm a mean sonofabitch and I'm not afraid of croaking.

THE MAN
    Listen. Stop that. I didn't do anything to you. I can give you
    money but a man has to be alive to go to his bank or write a
    cheque a man who's alive can make you rich while a dead man
    can only give you trouble.

JO
    How much?

THE MAN
    Pardon me?

JO
    How much for your life?

THE MAN
    Let's say–

JO
    No.

THE MAN
    I didn't say anything.

JO
    I want triple that.

THE MAN
    Fine. Quadruple if you want.

JO
    No. I like putting people out of their misery as an act of charity.
    And you are clearly in misery... You know the story of the bum
    who goes into this rich guy's house and the rich bastard tells him
    not to spit on the floor like he usually does because of the carpets

and the precious hardwood floors and the whole luxury kit and caboodle and would you believe it the other guy happened to have a big gob all ready in his mouth just waiting to get out a gob takes up a lot of space in your mouth and you have to get rid of it because swallowing it no he'd swallowed enough crap in his life that old geezer standing there loaded down with the gob in his mouth in the middle of the rich guy's house so he spit in the rich guy's face saying it was the only dirty place in the house...

Funny same for me it's not particularly clean here not really a rich guy's house but...

He spits in his face. The man wipes his face with his sleeve.

So what have you come here for? Watch out I'm not the chick the pretty little waif wasn't so tough was she? But I'm empty.

He grabs the man by the collar of his overcoat. He passes his switchblade lightly over the man's neck but the man doesn't flinch. JO doesn't press hard but a bit of blood appears on the man's neck.

The Reaper's first caress sir.

THE MAN
Please put that blade away. You'll end up really hurting yourself. You and I are forged from the same metal me the owner and you the beggar both violently opposed to all change and to all innovative disruption. Both of us well established me in opulence and you in destitution.

JO
Big talker eh big talker.
Go ahead maestro con artist go ahead or I'll slit your throat go ahead find the words make me come make me moan maestro.

And since you need reasons try these: thou shalt take one ram
and thou shalt slay the ram an offering for the sins of thy people.
So now give us your answer or you're dead: what did you come
here for?

THE MAN
My son.

JO
What?

THE MAN
I came here looking for my son.

JO
Well then you should've said so earlier of course our man is
risking his life for the flesh of his flesh so the dear boy left his
comfy home to lose himself in this forest of hyenas. Maybe he's a
drug addict? There's no such thing as children these days so who
is the nice young heir? What is the young man's name? Does he
have any idea that you are in the vicinity searching for him?

THE MAN
I'm not saying any more. Help me you won't regret it. 100,000
now payable in cash at any bank and 100,000 once I've found him.

JO
You're going to be my ram and not like that other guy the Father's
asshole sacrificed to save the world no with you it's just for hate
just for the pleasure it'll give me just to get my rocks off so my
come can mix with your spilt blood.

*He raises the switchblade very high. Miko bolts out of the shadows
behind Jo's back and knocks him out with a plank.*

THE MAN
    Thank you.

MIKO
    Don't say thank you all the time it bugs me.

THE MAN
    I owe you for that.

MIKO
    I'm not asking for anything. I don't want anything from you.
    You're not the one I'm protecting it's him. I'm protecting him
    from himself. He'd fuck up all the time if I wasn't around to stop
    him once in a while.
    He crushed the platinum watch. Your watch. Stomped on it. It
    was a beautiful watch.

THE MAN
    If I get out of here alive I'll buy you all the watches you want.

MIKO
    Don't count on me to help you. It's not a watch or a regiment of
    watches that could convince me to do anything for you.

The man exits.

13

JO, MIKO

Miko is putting a bandage on Jo's head.

MIKO
Don't touch me. It hurts when you touch me.

JO
I'm tired Miko.

MIKO
I thought you were a tornado but you tire you're losing it.

JO
Fuck you.

MIKO
Up high as a kite one minute down the next. You're polar. Reversible.

JO
Is your mind really silent as a grave?

MIKO
I never say nothing to nobody Jo.

JO
You know that you and me are a new race. A race of metaphysical hallucinatory apotheosis.

MIKO
You alright?

JO

> We fart in the face of death. We know that the blah-blah-blah
> and the cash are for the rest of them. You look beautiful like that
> in the slats casting a ladder of light. You like this place?

MIKO

> Never saw such a shitty place.

JO

> Sometimes there are moments when I feel a kind of amazement
> at having been alive. While you were talking to that pretty pig
> with the swollen pink teats I was talking to the old man. You
> know who that old man is? You know who he's looking for here?

Beat.

MIKO

> When you stop talking like that it's not a good sign. There's
> always something outrageous in your silence.

JO

> That old man who looks so straight in reality–

MIKO

> I don't want to hear about the old geezer. He's got fuck all to do
> with us. Leave him alone let him go. Stop–

JO

> He's looking for his son here.

MIKO

> Oh. So? That's his problem.

JO

> You think so buddy. Nobody's ever safe from loneliness. There

will always be the lonely ones and the others: two enemy camps. Sometimes one lonely type kidnaps another and together they escape to the other camp. Never any violent confrontations or any clear decisions but always this very visible border between the lonely ones and the others. The two camps exchange hostages and the old man's come to get his so he can finally leave the camp of loneliness. And the hostage he's come for is you.

MIKO

Me!

JO

You never told me about your father.

MIKO

Nothing to say–

JO

You see. This man who tames the bears and boars of his bank has come here to lay himself at your feet like a little puppy. So now it's all up to you Miko. What are you going to extract from the guy?

MIKO

I don't have a father. And that's one thing that can't change.

JO

It can change. From one day to the next it can change. The proof. It's about to change.

MIKO

No. I don't have a father. A mountain of muscles or a thousand soldiers couldn't change that.

JO

> You're not hearing me. We're in a desert and nobody understands anybody. I don't give a shit that you don't have a father. I'm telling you that he's looking for a son and with your pretty little wild angel face you'll fill the bill just fine and you're going to fuck off with him–

MIKO

> What about us?

JO

> It's all over you and me. We won't be saying goodnight to each other anymore goodnight around here is a lie anyway all the nights around here are bad.

MIKO

> It's his son he's looking for not just anybody who can play son.

JO

> I'm telling you it will work.

MIKO

> I got a complaint Jo. What are you up to? Don't you want us to see each other anymore?

JO

> You're a barbarian Miko and I know what barbarians are like barbarians are looking for pleasure and I'm offering you wall-to-wall pleasure.

MIKO

> Don't try to patch up irreparable things it won't work. There's a big hole in the middle of your scenario. If the man's come here looking for his son that means his son is around here somewhere he's not the type to strike out without a compass he's got his sources and if his son is around here it must be–

JO
Do you sometimes forget to mind your own business?

The man has appeared.

Silence.

Miko exits.

PART III

14

JO, THE MAN

THE MAN
   Do you find this interesting?

JO
   I got a splitting headache.

THE MAN
   It will go away.

JO
   Give me back my blade.

THE MAN
   They should behead us fast before old age and the ailments in
   our sleep or at the edge of the woods when we arrive at the train
   station one morning attacked by some masks and crack...
   One day my wife left me taking the kids with her. Never heard
   from her again.
   One day I tracked them down: my wife dead in a psychiatric
   ward years after she left me. I know I seem like a total bastard or
   a coward. One day I tracked down this son–

JO
   Give my switchblade back to me.

THE MAN

I don't really feel like having my throat slit by some punk.

JO

Give it back.

THE MAN

That's like asking the snow to fall sooner. I didn't come here to catch my death.

JO

You look at me and you say to yourself: "This guy has no thoughts he only has impulses." I won't use the knife on you again. I'm no longer afraid of you I don't want anything from you you're not asking me for anything either total indifference that's the exact feeling between us and that's the feeling I prefer.

THE MAN

Perhaps. Strange but I knew the minute I saw you that you and I were of the same race perfectly capable of understanding each other.

JO

Nobody on this earth ever cared if I was dead or alive.

THE MAN

I'd like our meeting to be a success I'd say to him: "I could if you want help you now in your adult life."

JO

That's crap. What man can make a man of his child? If my father ever found me again what could I say to him except: "Leave me in my fuckup."

This is where the reign of your police and your kings stops
and when the kings no longer know how to reign the masses
get restless.
Give me back my switchblade.

THE MAN

If I were standing before this son I would say to him: "Of course
I never helped you learn to do divisions with decimal points or–"

JO

Poetry hot air and nonsense.
All fathers are bastards to their sons. If he was standing before
me now I'd tell him: "It's too late grandad. The demons have
entered my mouth all seven orifices of my head and they're
gnawing on my brain from inside. They're staging a fiesta in my
belly and they're chipping away at my skull so they can sow their
sick shit. I don't expect anything anymore I expected for so long
I used up all my expectation."

THE MAN

I can't talk like you. I never really loosened the gag on my mouth
and that's part of my problem. But if I had him here–

JO

Are you going to give me the blade?

THE MAN

Wouldn't he feel that this meeting is not a demand or a settling
of who knows what bad debt between us but a let's say gratuitous
way of seeing each other again and telling each other...
Would you refuse the money I could give you just like that for
no reason asking for absolutely nothing in return?

JO

Money it's possible and impossible so why not money?

THE MAN

And if you... (*Suddenly Jo leaps behind the man's back and twists his arm into a judo hold. He searches the man's pockets, takes out a wad of bills and retrieves his switchblade.*) I was going to give it all to you.

JO

Taking is much better. Don't have to say thanks. The son would also tell you that he can stand everything except affection.

The man exits.

15

SARAH, JO, MIKO then THE MAN

Miko is holding Jo in check with the switchblade he undoubtedly pinched from him. Sarah, his accomplice.

SARAH
   We're not asking for much are we Jo? You used to be a real nice guy Jo. A bit hard to control as a kid the nervous type rebellious unreliable you skipped school. Quickly placed in a home–

JO
   Glue acetone–

MIKO (*playing along*)
   Shooting up alcohol.

JO
   Then valium and pentothal...

He laughs.

SARAH
   Kind of a nice kid baker then docker set up in a bachelor and classified as a young adult–

MIKO
   I bet you didn't even know what that meant?

JO
   What are you two getting at?

MIKO

We're stirring up painful memories.

SARAH

Loads of memories that refuse to die...
A whole army of counsellors would come snooping into your
business every so often in that sinister neighbourhood with the
steep hills those flights of slippery stairs the dark passageways
the alleys full of stinking garbage that horizon a cold slab of tin
the grid of dry docks and warehouses nothing but doors nailed
shut with planks abandoned quays decaying buildings filled with
squatters and you a quiet little guy yes quiet nothing special...

JO

She doesn't know what she's saying Miko.

MIKO

The truth you've always been afraid of women. Stop laughing
like that for god's sake.

JO

It's nerves. Seeing the two of you gang up on me...

MIKO

You're wrong to go on hiding him. If you don't give him back
he'll die.

JO

Miko please enough.

SARAH

We'll stop whenever you want.

JO

Remember that bar Miko? You kept watching me you were acting like you didn't see me but you were watching I'd change place you'd search for me with your eyes... (*He notices the man.*) Where'd he crawl out from? Under the rocks like a snake?

Sarah takes a drink.

Leave some for me.

SARAH

Just one sip (*she takes another*) just one. The bottle's empty.

MIKO

Tell us where you're hiding him? Nothing to say? Still not talking?

SARAH

One night you went the distance you stuck a spike in an old drunk's throat and you ran off because someone was coming. You've been running all your life Jo. Everything I'm saying must be coming back to you bit by bit right?

MIKO

You said you told me everything Jo that I was your memory and I didn't know anything–

JO

You won't get anywhere this way stupid. Acting like you're God or the devil you think you know everything you know nothing.

SARAH

Tell us where you're hiding the little bundle who's stopped crying now who's sleeping who's cold and hasn't eaten. Tell us Jo and we'll leave you alone.

MIKO

Tell us Jo. I don't want to know all this shit about you I already
know enough and if you don't talk she won't stop...

Jo remains silent.

SARAH

Some minutes become a huge gap... Now you're going to learn
something else about your old buddy Jo... One night you went
back to the old folks' place.

JO

Stop her Miko please make her shut up. Both of you stop.

He laughs nervously.

SARAH

Your old caretakers who'd been kicking themselves since the day
they rescued you from the mess where your real parents had the
good sense to dump you right at birth and they're more or less
happy to see you again they hardly looked up from the telly what
do you have to do to get them to see you five years since they
saw you living barely five miles away...
The kid sister was asleep you went to sit on the edge of her bed
no way you could recognize her five years later...
So that night the old folks were snoring and you got up in the
room full of kids' toys and stuffed animals even though the girl
was beyond the toy age and you put your hand over her mouth
to prevent her from screaming and you–

JO

Liar.
Don't listen to her Miko she's lying.
I can't remember my sister...

Miko is crying, his head between his legs. Jo laughs nervously.

THE MAN (*picking up the switchblade*)
Enough of this game.

JO
We're not talking to you. Go away. You're not from here.

MIKO
Sarah...

SARAH
Shut up little jerk.

Sarah goes over to Jo. She wipes his face with a handkerchief. Loving gestures.

You alright Jo? You OK?

JO
I'm fine. Untie me Miko my wrists hurt.

Miko spits in his face. Sarah unties Jo. Jo picks up the empty bottle and breaks it over his own head.

I'm fine Sarah. Just great.

Miko runs off. The man walks off slowly.

16

JO, SARAH then MIKO then THE MAN

JO

You're not fighting with human weapons. You're trying to bite devour rip to shreds. There's only one solution: hunt you down and slaughter you.

SARAH

You think I'm a nun? You kidnap my kid.

JO

Our kid. I'll be a good father Sarah I swear a real good father.

SARAH

You start by stealing his mother from him by starving him to death by abandoning him in some place where anybody could–

JO

No way Sarah he's safe where he is besides it's not even raining–

SARAH

He's going to die dumb shit if you don't give him back to me–

JO

He's safe from the draughts and the rats in a cement drainpipe–

SARAH

You think that's all he needs safe from the rats and the draughts you've got draughts in your head why did you steal that kid from me Jo?

JO

I'll be a good father Sarah I swear–

SARAH

Let me feed him first idiot let me help him grow a·bit idiot before
he can share your crazy shit. I won't even have to give him back
to you one day he'll turn to you that's how it is the young male
runs to his father one fine day as soon as the male hormones
take over but first he has to grow a few years gain a little weight
some brain some muscle by feeding off his mother's weaknesses
that's how it works even in the wild idiot.

JO

You'll give him back to me once you've spoiled him rotten is
that it?

SARAH

I won't give him back to you Jo he'll come back on his own
and it will be better that way for both of you but it will take a
while still.

JO

You never wanted this kid right?

SARAH

Don't make things complicated Jo. Hurry up. Go get him.

JO

I wear kneepads leg pads wristbands to support my failing bones
that are just waiting for a chance to let me down... Just like you
Sarah you've let me down...

SARAH

Don't touch me.

JO

He's a burden anyway I don't know what to do with that little bundle he cries and can't stop peeing on himself.

SARAH

No wonder. It's beyond your field of expertise Jo.

JO

You have to choose: him or Miko. You can't have everything.

SARAH

What would I do with Miko? I've got enough on my hands with one kid.

JO

He hasn't been the same since he met you.

SARAH

That's your fault if you hadn't stolen the kid your precious Miko never would have met me.

JO

Okay you win Sarah anyway the poker game is over with the old man and I don't even know who won and I don't know what to do with that little bundle that cries and can't stop peeing on himself.

He exits. He returns with the bundle of blankets wrapped around the child. Sarah takes the child.

SARAH

You deserve to have me fuck off and leave you here now. You're just a child. A child made me a child.

JO

> Never say that to Miko you hear me?
> Some day I'll convert to peyote everything turns green and is shaped like a cactus your skin turns green with little bags under your eyes and presto you start looking like the oldest Indian in the world... In case of an overdose you die with the same symptoms as polio but if you survive it's total detox.

Miko enters.

MIKO

> Did he give him back? What did you do so he'd give him back? Did you sleep with him?

SARAH

> We made this kid together. Might not be our greatest achievement but we did it.

MIKO

> Oh.

Beat.

JO

> Shut up Sarah. Don't listen to her Miko she doesn't know what she's saying.

MIKO

> You two really tricked me didn't you? And now what? What about little Miko use once and destroy?

JO

> Calm down.

MIKO

You don't care about me any more than she does do you? I hate you Sarah. Why didn't you ever tell me Jo?

The man enters.

THE MAN

You're fighting like blind animals in the dark incapable of agreeing upon a definition of the sun...

MIKO

The kid's not moving. He's not moving.

THE MAN

We have to warm him up. (*The man massages the baby.*) He's alive. But if we don't hurry–

SARAH

I'm not scared I'm not scared.

THE MAN

He's too exhausted to react. Come with me. Let's get to a hospital.

SARAH

And bodies always beget bodies flesh makes flesh. Aren't I warm enough to put life back into his body?

THE MAN

No.

MIKO

You're nuts Jo you're–

SARAH

I don't want to go there. They'll take him away from me their social workers will say I can't keep him they'll take him away from me–

THE MAN

Don't act like a baby. If we don't do something soon it will be too late. You prefer a dead baby?

SARAH

If I go there they'll take him away from me.

THE MAN

And if you stay here he'll die. Let's go. Come.

SARAH

I don't know what to do.

THE MAN

I'll buy this child from you. I'll write you a cheque a hundred thousand you can cash it today. It can get you out of this mess. And maybe the child can be saved and have a good life. And you can have other children later.

SARAH

You're a smooth sonofabitch.

THE MAN

It's possible... Everything is possible...
Two hundred thousand. Hurry up in fifteen minutes I'll withdraw my offer because it will be too late to save him.

MIKO

Don't listen to him Sarah.

SARAH
  Three hundred.

THE MAN
  Two hundred and fifty that's my final offer.

SARAH
  Three hundred.

THE MAN
  You're playing Russian roulette. I said two hundred and fifty.

SARAH
  It's a deal. Two hundred and fifty.

The man signs a cheque. Sarah passes him the child. The man hurries off.

MIKO
  Sarah?

SARAH
  Get away from me ok?

JO
  Everybody steps on everybody's toes and nobody worries about
  who he's crushing...

MIKO
  Where are you going Sarah? Wait for me I'm coming with you.

JO
  No way.

SARAH

You two can kill each other now I don't give a shit! I couldn't care less.

She exits.

17

JO, MIKO then SARAH

MIKO
   We could've shared that girl.

JO
   Don't be morbid. All women would have broken your heart.

Sarah returns and goes over to Jo. They look at each other.

MIKO
   You are my only real buddy. I don't think I'll ever have another
   one like you before I check out. Don't leave me Jo. The unbelievable
   wreck of my life. How to jump over this open cesspit.

Sarah kisses Jo.

JO
   Enough to kill a guy honest.

MIKO
   Jo. You are my brother my friend not my demon. Think of those
   two-bit whores the ugliest the oldest fleabag whores. Jo. (*Jo kisses
   Miko.*) Enough to kill a guy honest.
   Jo. We can fight our way out of this hole. I watch you stumble
   around in the dark. Why do I feel so...? This steel this cement
   this asphalt these railroad bridges crossing these canals the
   boxing matches the brown smoky halls. Jo.

JO

Stop complaining that God didn't make you grander.

MIKO

I'm not complaining I feel like a drunk nigger banging on a trash can in the fog...

Sarah slips off.

JO

Why do I feel so good? I'll tell you each and every one of my fears... Sarah? Where did Sarah go?

MIKO

We're going to hit the road together you and me Jo like two men take me in your arms Jo shake off your fucking mushy despair Jo stop look over there in the middle of the clouds in the desert of nightfall...

JO (*shouting*)
SARAAAAH!

MIKO

That's the huge finger of their sonafabitchin God Jo his index finger pointing at us through the coal dust and the gloom of snow.

JO

Find her Miko find her.

MIKO

Stop bleating like that in the dark Jo. Once it's gone it never comes back the world is old and we're even older you and me and her. Look the first rays of a new morning–

JO

SARAAAH!

MIKO

You are by far the only great man I've ever known.

JO

SARAAAH!

MIKO

Jo. Do you think it's possible to go on living here?

FINAL BLACKOUT

Written at La Chartreuse
October 1993–May 1994

About the playwright:

Michel Azama's plays have been translated into 15 languages and produced all over the world. They include: *Le Sas, Vie et Mort de Pier Paolo Pasolini, Bled, Croisades, Iphigénie ou le Péché des dieux, Saintes familles (a trilogy), Voyage vers le centre* and *Médée black*.

Zoo de nuit received the prestigious Prix Beaumarchais and, in 1999, Michel Azama was awarded the *Grand prix de la ville de Bourges* for his body of work .

Michel Azama is the president of the Écrivains associés de théâtre (EAT) and the founder and editor-in-chief of the *Cahiers de Prospéro*. He recently edited a three-volume anthology of plays by contemporary French playwrights entitled *De Godot à Zucco* (éditions Théâtrales).

About the translator:

Linda Gaboriau has translated some 70 plays, including the works of some of Québec's most prominent playwrights. Her translations of plays by Michel Marc Bouchard, René-Daniel Dubois, Normand Chaurette, Daniel Danis, Michel Garneau, Gratien Gélinas, Jovette Marchessault, Wajdi Mouawad and Michel Tremblay have been published and widely produced across Canada and abroad. She has won the Governor General's Award for Translation (in 1996, for her translation of *Stone and Ashes* by Daniel Danis) and three Chalmers Awards.

Ms. Gaboriau has also worked as a free lance journalist and broadcaster. She has a longstanding association with Montreal's Centre des auteurs dramatiques (CEAD) where she directed the play development program and coordinated numerous translation and international exchange activities. For several years, she was an associate director of the Banff playRites Colony (in charge of translation projects) and is currently the director of the Banff International Literary Translation Centre.

BABY STAIN

(P'tite Souillure)

By Koffi Kwahulé

Translated by
David Homel

Production Information:

P'tite Souillure was first produced in 2002 at the Festival de Frictions in Dijon, France, and was directed by Serge Tranvouez. The same year, it went on to win the prestigious Journées d'Auteurs prize in Lyons.

Baby Stain was workshopped and read at the 2001 Banff playRites Colony.

Acknowledgements:

Acknowledgements and thanks to Rodney St-Eloi for the Haitian Creole song.

In memory of Robert MacLeod
Koné Ibrahima
Jean-Claude Grenier

You have to leave home behind to find it.
– Ralph Ellison

In the human world, there are three times.
The time to speak,
The time to act,
The time to see.
So, when the day comes when words must be spoken,
Announce!
When the day comes when the thing must be done,
Act!
And when the day comes to examine it all,
Add it up!
For the human world there are three times.
– Baba Sissoka, *griot*

For nothing is secret that shall not be made manifest;
Neither any thing hid, that shall not be known
and come abroad
–Luke, 8:17

Night. A middle-class house. Mother, father, daughter.

*A screen, perhaps a giant television screen. The father is trying in vain
to isolate an image from* **Gone with the Wind** *(or some similar film).
As the image flickers past, we catch the famous kiss shared by Clark
Gable and Viven Leigh.*

*Meanwhile, in the opening in the back wall (about the size of a garage
door), a mask dances to no music, an airy, light, drifting dance, as if in
slow motion.*

*Only the mother sees the dancing mask, though she does not pay it
much attention, as if it were a familiar image.*

*The scene titles are not part of the spoken text. There are no breaks
between the scenes; the action of the play is to be performed as one
continuous movement.*

FATHER: *(trying to isolate the image, almost to himself, the way a
    person hums a tune in the shower, barely audible)*
    In those days... In those days Babylon... Baby... lon... Baby...
    Babylon was burying Nebu... Nebuchad... Nebuchad...
    Nebuchad... Nebuchadnezzar... was burying Nebuchadnezzar. On
    the banks... the banks of the Eu... phra... tes... on the banks of
    the Euphrates, from the left bank to the right... in all
    Mesopotamia... Me... so... po... ta... mia... *(stops on the image)*
    Look, dear, that's us.

*The mask disappears. Someone is ringing the doorbell. Immediately the
father switches off the image as if he had been caught in a forbidden
act. Silence.*

MOTHER:
Who is it? *(another ring)* Go see who it is!

DAUGHTER:
It's okay, Papa, I'll go.

The bell is insistent.

FATHER:
Ask who it is before you open the door.

DAUGHTER:
Who is it?

VOICE BEHIND THE DOOR:
It's me.

MOTHER:
Who?

VOICE BEHIND THE DOOR:
Me.

DAUGHTER:
He says it's him.

MOTHER:
That's absurd! Who's him?

The daughter opens the door and a young man appears.

INTRUDER:
Who does that red car out front belong to?

DAUGHTER:
Ikedia!

IKEDIA:
  ...descended from lightning, come to burn down this house.

Shocked silence. Ikedia bursts out laughing.

DAUGHTER:
  He's laughing, Mama. Ikedia! Papa, it's Ikedia!

MOTHER:
  Ikedia?

FATHER:
  Ikedia... Ikedia... Ikedia...

DAUGHTER:
  Of course it's Ikedia. Come with me, Ikedia.

MOTHER AND FATHER:
  Pleased to meet you.

DAUGHTER:
  Papa...

IKEDIA:
  Pleased to meet you.

DAUGHTER:
  Mama...

IKEDIA:
  Pleased to meet you.

FATHER:
  So it's you?

IKEDIA:

I guess so.

DAUGHTER:

He's my Ikedia.

IKEDIA:

It's a beautiful evening. The sky is clear and the moon is bright. (*silence*) A perfect night, wouldn't you say?

FATHER:

Yes, yes... perfect... Of course... As you say.... Perfect... perfect.... So, finally, we meet.

DAUGHTER:

That's my Ikedia! Showing up, just like that! Isn't he handsome, Papa?

FATHER:

He couldn't be better. I hope you'll be staying for supper.

IKEDIA:

I came for supper.

FATHER:

Excellent, we're completely delighted. Care for something?

IKEDIA:

A glass of Condrieu.

MOTHER:

Really?

FATHER:

And you, dear?

MOTHER: *(to her daughter)*
   We have to talk... Nothing for me.

The mother searches for something.

IKEDIA:
   There, over there, they're right there. *(the mother grabs a vial of pills)* Isn't that what you were looking for?

She gulps down several pills. Silence.

FATHER:
   So, you're Ikedia?

IKEDIA:
   I guess so.

MOTHER:
   We have to talk...

FATHER:
   "I guess so" – how charming!

IKEDIA:
   Nice yard you've got.

MOTHER:
   What?

IKEDIA:
   The garden – magnificent, just like Eden.

MOTHER:
   I'm the one with the green thumb. I drew up the plans, I planted everything.

IKEDIA:

A treat for the senses.

MOTHER:

At least someone has some taste.

DAUGHTER:

You'll see tomorrow, it's even prettier during the day.

FATHER:

Ah! Because you're... *(hands him the glass)* Here.

DAUGHTER:

Do I have bad breath or something?

FATHER:

What?

DAUGHTER:

The same as Ikedia.

MOTHER:

Tell me, you're not...

DAUGHTER:

Of course he's staying. He's sleeping in my room tonight.

MOTHER:

Oh! *(to her daughter)* We have to talk...

IKEDIA:

I know how to behave myself.

DAUGHTER:

See, Mother, I wasn't making things up when I told you about Ikedia.

FATHER:

Our daughter is right. You're obviously well brought up, well educated... And what a sense of humor! That business about the son of lightning, come to burn down the house – it was delightfully incongruous.

MOTHER:

This is absurd! The way I remember it, you told us Ikedia had a slight cast in his eye, as far as I remember.

DAUGHTER:

Of course, Mother, didn't you see his eyes?

FATHER:

"I have come to burn down..." – very charming, really.

MOTHER:

Yes... but...

FATHER:

However, and I hope you won't take offence...

DAUGHTER:

He does! A very slight cast...

FATHER:

You've only just arrived...

DAUGHTER:

I bet you never looked into his eyes...

FATHER:

... And already I come at you with this...

MOTHER:

I looked at his eyes...

FATHER:
But one thing intrigues me...

MOTHER:
I saw them very well.

FATHER:
You understand, our daughter has talked so much about you... about Ikedia, that I'm sure that...

DAUGHTER:
Ikedia, show my mother your eyes.

FATHER:
Do you like Caravaggio?

IKEDIA:
Cara...?

FATHER:
Caravaggio. (*Italian accent*) Il Caravaggio?

DAUGHTER:
Go ahead, take a good look.

IKEDIA:
Il...

MOTHER:
I saw them all right.

IKEDIA:
Oh, yes, the... Yes, of course... It depends.

DAUGHTER:
Don't be jealous of my happiness.

FATHER:

Unless you prefer Bacon?

IKEDIA:

Bacon?

MOTHER:

He doesn't have a cast... He doesn't have a cast.

FATHER:

Bacon? Francis Bacon?

DAUGHTER:

Sure he does, take a closer look.

FATHER:

Good old Frank...

DAUGHTER:

Those eyes! Like rainbows!

IKEDIA:

Oh, him? Like my mother says, you have to take the good with the bad.

MOTHER:

That's absurd! He can't have rainbow eyes...

FATHER:

On the other hand, he had baroque tendencies too...

DAUGHTER:

He has a rainbow in his eyes.

FATHER:

... From a certain point of view.

MOTHER:

I didn't see any rainbow in his eyes.

IKEDIA:

Yes. From a certain point of view...

MOTHER:

And no cast either. None at all.

FATHER:

Since his death, the prices haven't stopped climbing.

DAUGHTER:

At least look at them!

FATHER:

On the other hand, even while he was alive.

DAUGHTER:

Ikedia, show her your eyes.

FATHER:

But it's taken on such proportions... A little like Basquiat!

DAUGHTER:

See, he has rainbow eyes.

MOTHER:

He absolutely does not.

FATHER:

Do you like Basquiat?

IKEDIA:

Why should I like all those people?

FATHER:

See, dear, another one who doesn't like Basquiat.

MOTHER:

Ah, you don't either? I think he's overrated, but what can you do... Though my husband does see a certain sense of movement in his work...

FATHER:

But in general he's rather coarse, with that adolescent sense of rebellion, childish, I'd have to say...

MOTHER:

My husband is a painter, you understand...

FATHER:

Not exactly, I'm more of a Sunday painter. And even then...

MOTHER:

Now don't start up with that... One day he'll suffocate on his own modesty.

DAUGHTER: (*showing the paintings on the wall*)
These things on the wall, he did them.

MOTHER:

What do you think? For me there's something instinctive... something... oh, you know! He's a real artist! That perpetual flight of the senses! And so visionary!

FATHER:

I commit a few canvases from time to time. These accidents, on the wall... Of course it's not Basquiat, let alone Caravaggio, but what can you do... Actually, I'm a doctor...

IKEDIA:
  I know.

FATHER:
  Of course, my daughter must have told you...

IKEDIA:
  I know – I just know.

MOTHER:
  I see!

DAUGHTER:
  Ikedia knows everything. Coming, Ikedia?

FATHER:
  Our daughter has told us so much about... about Ikedia that I
  could draw his portrait from memory.

IKEDIA:
  That much?

FATHER:
  That much. On the other hand, sir... I know it might appear
  untoward, even shocking –

DAUGHTER:
  Ikedia, this is pissing me off!

FATHER:
  ... but as soon as I heard our daughter speak your name, Ikedia's
  features began to fade from my memory. At first I didn't notice
  that you weren't –

MOTHER:

Let me take care of this. Now, young man, would you mind reassuring me... I suppose you've never had rainbow eyes?

IKEDIA:

See for yourself.

MOTHER:

You're not Ikedia.

DAUGHTER:

He is Ikedia!

IKEDIA:

What difference does it make who I am? My name is Ikedia and I've come to burn down this house. Isn't that good enough for you?

He bursts out laughing again.

DAUGHTER:

He's laughing, Mama, he's laughing. Look, look how he's laughing!

FATHER:

I wasn't mistaken. You're very well educated and you have an excellent sense of humor. I know I really have no right to ask this of you, but for our daughter's sake, would you mind continuing to play the role of Ikedia, just for this one night?

DAUGHTER:

Who says he's playing? Come on, Ikedia, I'll show you my room.

MOTHER:

Your bag... May I take your bag?

IKEDIA:

No, don't bother... You can take it later... When I won't need it any more.

Ikedia and the daughter exit.

MOTHER:

Actually, the red car is mine. It was my car. It hasn't moved for years, except in my nightmares.

Like a Rutting Beast

MOTHER:

It's him.

FATHER:

You think so?

MOTHER:

It's him, all right.

FATHER:

But who is he?

MOTHER:

A week ago I found a pot of amaryllis that had been knocked over, and peonies that had been cruelly trampled. Right away I thought of her because of the browallias. But now I know it was him. The day before yesterday I was sure I heard someone in the garden, at night. I said to myself it was an alley cat, or some kind of animal... He's spoiled the garden all right, but that doesn't mean he's Ikedia. Even with rainbow eyes he couldn't be Ikedia. But he is someone.

FATHER:

Maybe it was a cat after all.

MOTHER:

No, no... it was him. I didn't pay much attention at the time. Everything happened so fast... Too fast... Her window. The noise that night was coming from her window... I should have... How many nights has he been visiting her in her bed?

FATHER:

He admitted it... almost... almost. Between the lines... He admitted it in so many words.

MOTHER:

And?

FATHER:

He came to burn down the house.

MOTHER:

I don't believe it... It's absurd! She's making fools of us. She's pulling our leg, she's making monkeys of us. Good Lord, what is she going to come up with next?

FATHER:

Don't get excited! You saw me, I made him promise to go easy on her, and make her think he really is Ikedia. So get a hold of yourself.

MOTHER:

Now I'm sure, those noises in the garden the other night – that was him! That was him. That's why he's been prowling around this house like a rutting beast. Because of her smell. When she's in that state you could smell that smell of... of... that warm smell of... to the very ends of the earth... To the very ends of the earth!

FATHER:

Don't start up again!

MOTHER:

What are you going to do about it?

FATHER:

For the time being, nothing. Just keep calm. Have you ever met him before?

MOTHER:

Good Lord, of course not! I've never seen him in my life.

FATHER:

Think about it, think hard. At the bakery, at the smoke shop, in the street... anywhere... think hard. Maybe without intending to, you might have said something to him... that he could have interpreted as an insult... A sidelong glance... sometimes just a look... Because you don't show up at someone's house for holiday dinner just to see how the turkey is doing!

MOTHER:

I'm telling you her smell drew him here. Unless... oh, my God! But there's nothing worth stealing here... I could give him the few jewels I have... I'll give him everything, but then he's got to go, he has to clear out of here!

FATHER:

Get a hold of yourself.

MOTHER:

I want you to kick him out! I want you to throw him right out the door!

FATHER:

Calm down, dear, please calm down. I've thought of it. But you
mustn't rush things. This type of individual is capable of using
any pretext to... Let's be a little subtle, shall we?

MOTHER:

His bag... did you see his bag? He didn't want me to touch it.
Right away he stiffened about his bag. He stiffened... That's
absurd! A proper person doesn't go visiting people that way, with
a bag slung over his shoulder. I told you to kick him out! Or do
you want me to do it?

FATHER:

No, I'll look after it.

Ikedia

In the girl's room.
She shows him her suitcase, already packed.

DAUGHTER:

See, I'm ready. I've been waiting for you for years. For weeks I've
been listening for you in the song of the trees in the garden, and
then, the other day, from my window, I saw your eyes light up in
the night, in the middle of the Chinese jasmine. Is it true you're
the son of lightning? I'm sure she's giving him all kinds of big
ideas about you. "Kick him out! I want you to throw him out!"
But you won't stand for it, will you? Promise me you'll have the
balls to stand up to her. Anyway, it doesn't matter, we're leaving.
If you only knew what a drag they are! But now you've come. I
always imagined you'd come on horseback. A white horse with
black spots, like a Dalmatian. You on your Dalmatian horse.
Riding up. From behind. I've always seen you from behind,

Ikedia. One day I was in a city I don't remember its name with my parents one of those places you've never seen but you have the feeling you've lived there a long time ago in another life. You were on a motorcycle. A girl was driving the motorcycle her hair was floating in the wind I thought she's happy Ikedia makes a woman happy. Without dismounting you tear me away from the family supper, you tear me away from the family council, you tear me away from the family outing, you tear me away from the family order, you tear me away from the family circle, you tear me away without dismounting. The horse like a Dalmatian spreads its rainbow wings. Two rainbows shatter the family burden, they punish the air, they split the clouds. Is it true what they say? That thunder is the climax of the clouds? *(she imitates thunder)* Then an orgasm, and another one *(she imitates thunder)*! And an ejaculation, and another one! Is it true or isn't it, son of lightning? *(she changes her clothes)* Turn around! I won't look at you and you won't see me. *(a beat)* Somewhere in here there's the rotting body of a mask, and the very soul of this house is sick with it. Lots of times I wanted to burn down this place and take off, but I don't hate my father enough to do that. *(a beat)* But you'll hate him. I'm sure you'll hate him, you won't just hate him, you'll despise him. When he starts rolling those big eyes of his like a puppy dog that'll do anything to hold on to its bone, you'll despise him. It busted his balls the way she squealed on him to the whole city with those insinuations of hers about the pure thing that exists between him and me. *(a beat)* Tonight, when you tear me away from them after the fire, she won't understand why I'm leaving and I don't want her to understand I just want her to say to herself that it's absurd. That's what I want. It'll kill her not to know why I'm leaving, because they're supposed to be perfect parents who slave away to give me everything a girl could possibly dream of. Is it true you're the son of lightning? *(a pause)* Ikedia always enters back first, and you came in face first. No, don't turn around, stay that way so I can see you. I recognize people from their backs. You're not Ikedia. You know it and I know it.

IKEDIA: *(comes near the girl and caresses her absent-mindedly)*
Last night I came back.

DAUGHTER:
I know. This morning I had to pick up your cigarette butts.
Because of my parents.

IKEDIA:
Wear the panties you wore last night.

DAUGHTER:
You're not Ikedia. Ikedia is an I-don't-give-a-damn guy, the real
thing, with the hard-living look of a man who'd do it to you right
there on the seat in the last subway before they close it down.
Oh, no, you're not Ikedia. Ikedia is a sailor without a port who
tells life to go fuck itself every day of the year. Ikedia is a
mercenary with an albino's red eyes. Ikedia is a hired killer.
Ikedia is the hot wind on hard muscles like the impatient cock
that cornered me in the shithouse of some crummy dive one
night and left me with this. *(she takes the man's hand and strokes
her belly with it)* Now I know who you are. *(a beat)* You're not
Ikedia. Ikedia wouldn't have thought twice about slipping his
finger down there, where you'd just love to lose yourself but you
don't dare. You know why you're not Ikedia? Ikedia would have
slapped my mother back there. *(a beat)* Before I get out of here
I'm going to slap my mother. I've slapped her before. I'll slap her
again. Ikedia doesn't have a name. His name is nothing. Ikedia
wouldn't weigh himself down with a name, or any other baggage.

IKEDIA:
You're the reason I didn't burn down this place the very first
time. I wasn't even interested in you. I couldn't have imagined
that something like you could exist. The first time I came
here, it was because of the red car. Then I started coming back
every night.

DAUGHTER:
Ikedia wouldn't have come back every night, or even two nights in a row. Ikedia wouldn't have wailed away on my ass like some obsessed old pervert for seven whole nights, even if I did want it. The very first night, you would have smashed the glass and climbed through the window, and I would have called for help, and my father would have come running, and you would have sliced open his throat with a piece of glass. Then you would have laid me down like a sacrifice in my father's blood and you would have nailed me to the floor with your dick. That's what Ikedia would have done.

IKEDIA: (pulling the girl to him)
Watch your step. Watch what you say to me, Baby Stain.

DAUGHTER:
How about that, my father calls me Baby Stain too. How did you know?

IKEDIA:
I just know, that's all.

BABY STAIN:
"I just know, that's all." It's weird, you talk like a bad Hollywood movie. "I've come to burn down this house. Wear the panties you wore last night. Watch your step. I just know, that's all." A regular Hollywood movie! He's called me Baby Stain ever since I was a little girl. (a beat) You know that and you've got nothing to say?

IKEDIA:
Nothing.

BABY STAIN:
You sure are talkative! You say a couple of words then you shut

up, a couple more words then you shut up, but inside you're chattering away. The words keep piling up inside you, monologue without end, you're like a grave of words. Show me I'm wrong, show me that you're not as noisy as a graveyard. Or do what you came here to do and stop sputtering. *(he kisses her roughly)* Now you can tell me your real name... What is it? *(she grabs the revolver that Ikedia had on him)* Now you're Ikedia. You're completely Ikedia. So you weren't just bullshitting, you actually came here to kill us all and burn down the house.

IKEDIA:

I won't kill anyone.
I won't hang your mother
by her left eyelid
from the crescent moon.
I won't slit your father's throat
with a broken bottle,
and I won't rape you
in his blood.
When the time comes
I'll burn down this house
then I'll turn and walk away.
And that will be the end.

BABY STAIN:

The Hollywood movie again. Is it loaded? I'm going to do something stupid. I'm going to put a bullet in it. If I miss I'll get it instead. I hear it's no bigger than a tadpole. No bigger than that. For the time being. Now's the time to kill it. Because later it gets bigger, it gets fatter, it overflows and dances in your belly. Everyone can see it dancing in your belly. By then it's too late. Then I'll have to find Ikedia who's just a gust of wind that blew between my legs one night. I'll shoot where it came in... I saw that at the movies... Or maybe on TV... Unless I read about it... It was at the movies. Bang! Yeah, at the movies, I remember the noise, bang! And the blood! And the music flowing with the blood! This way I won't miss. Because it's as straight as a highway in there. On my back. Lie on my back so the highway runs straight. Bang! Right in the little bun-in-the-oven. *(he grabs the gun back from her)* What are you carrying around in that bag of yours? Come on, tell me! Let me have a little peek.

IKEDIA:

No.

BABY STAIN:

Come on, just with one eye. Open your bag for me, Ikedia!

IKEDIA:

No.
Inside is
pain that burns
from West to East,
blood that cries out
from earth to heaven,
and if I showed you
your eyes would be blinded,
and if I let you listen
your ears would be deafened.

BABY STAIN:

Wow! Now that's something! Something else! You're a regular one-man movie. Anyway I don't give a damn, I have no idea why you want to burn down this house and I don't care. I hope you don't have a reason, that's what I hope, I hope it's gratuitous, completely gratuitous. If you burn down the house, it'll be bad enough for her, this house is her whole life, and if she doesn't know why, well... I'm sure she'll have an attack. Fools always need a reason for things, it reassures them, it makes them feel secure, what do you want, they're fools. You were passing by you

saw the house you said to yourself I'm going to burn it down.
Why? Because. Because why? Because because. That would
definitely put her over the edge once and for all. I should have
burned it down when I was seven years old. (a beat) I'll wait a
few months till it makes its presence felt against the walls of my
belly and, ough! A knife right through its heart. Don't you want
to be the father of my child, Ikedia? Since you're the first one to
know? Ikedia doesn't know it yet, and he never will. Neither will
my mother. Or my father. (a beat) When it starts showing, if
those two downstairs bug me too much, I'll say it's my father's
fault. People will believe me. They'll believe me, no problem.
People always believe girls who accuse their fathers of that.
Especially around here. Ever since I was little he's called me Baby
Stain. It drives my mother crazy when he calls me Baby Stain. So
he doesn't call me Baby Stain when she's there. Around here
everyone knows I'm his little Baby Stain but they all act as if.
That's what this town is like. So people don't bother me. Otherwise,
the truth would make such a mess, nobody would get away
clean. We'd all have to go back to square one. Everyone on the
platform, all aboard! We're all starting from scratch! But before
that could happen, you showed up, the son of lightning, like a
terrible sign from above. Tell me, you're not just joking about
burning down this house?

IKEDIA:
Then I'll disappear, with you.

BABY STAIN:
You want to take me away?

IKEDIA:
So my heart can finally rest...

BABY STAIN:
You really want me? Come on, this time say something, let

yourself go, stop playing your Hollywood movie. Come on, Ikedia, open the prison of your heart, set your words free, let them soar into the sky and ease my waiting. Tell me something. Tell me, Ikedia. Do you love me?

IKEDIA:
Who's talking about love?

BABY STAIN:
Maybe just a little?

IKEDIA:
Baby Stain.

They kiss.

BABY STAIN:
Tell me again.

IKEDIA:
Baby Stain.

They kiss.

Re-enactment

The garden next to the house. A red couch stands in the grass. Ikedia is sitting on the couch holding a gun.

The music is both primitive and sophisticated, the meeting of several cultures. An example would be Coltrane's Alabama.

To this music, to the sound of the words of this song, the father is dancing the same airy, light, drifting dance from the beginning of the play.

FATHER:
  I am the chameleon mask
  I am the eldest son of creation
  In the beginning
  At the time of my birth
  There was nothing
  Earth had not yet been born
  In the immensity of primal emptiness
  Floated the fetus of the Earth
  The skin of the Earth was so fine
  That to walk
  I had only to brush its surface
  For fear of tearing it
  And from that time
  Was born my tentative gait
  I am the toad mask
  I am the eldest son of creation
  In the beginning
  At the time of my birth
  There was nothing
  Earth had not yet been born
  In the immensity of primal emptiness
  Floated a few stars of stone
  To make my way
  I jumped from rock to rock
  And from that time
  Was born my hopping gait
  I am the hornbill mask
  I am the eldest son of creation
  In the beginning
  At the time of my birth
  There was nothing
  Earth had not yet been born
  In the immensity of primal emptiness
  I floated alone

At my mother's death
Without fetus of earth or clod of soil
I split open my nose
To bury her there
And from that time
Was born the grave that sits upon my face.

Then he would start over, always the same story, the same dance.

IKEDIA: (aiming at the father)
   Was it like this?

FATHER:
   No. She was holding the gun this way, between her legs.

IKEDIA:
   Then what?

He gets off the couch.

FATHER:
   No, no, sit down. She didn't get out of the car. She fired from the window. (*Ikedia sits down and the father begins dancing again*) Now, fire! (*Ikedia aims at the father and fires. The father falls to the ground*)

IKEDIA:
   Then what? (*the father says nothing*) Then what?

FATHER:
   The Square emptied.

IKEDIA:
   And then?

FATHER:
The Square filled up again...

IKEDIA:
And then?

FATHER:
Around the body.

IKEDIA:
And then?

FATHER:
And then? And then?... Is that why you came here? You're a strange one after all. You show up with your "I've come to burn down this house," then you stop, not another normal word out of you, nothing, you don't say a thing, then all of a sudden it's "And then? And then?" I don't know... I don't have the answer... It's your turn.

IKEDIA:
When the time comes
I will speak
And the words I say
Will burst the eardrums of the world.

FATHER:
The day before yesterday you were here, under that tree, the acacia in the middle of the kalanchoes, beneath my daughter's window. You were here for a while, long enough to smoke two cigarettes. I picked up the butts because of my wife. She has no tolerance for the unexpected. She's always had heart problems and ever since the incident, she hasn't exactly been on an even keel.

IKEDIA:

And the days before that too. I needed to see the house from every angle. To weigh the fruit in my hand and come at it from every direction. Sooner or later the fruit will reveal, like an offering, the exact spot where the knife must be thrust in.

FATHER:

And did you find it?

IKEDIA:

Yes.
Now I know exactly
when the time comes
in which of the folds of this house
the match must be struck.

BABY STAIN'S VOICE:

Ikedia! Ikedia!

IKEDIA·

That's Baby Stain.

FATHER:

Ah! So she told you everything?

IKEDIA:

She didn't say anything. I just know, that's all.

FATHER:

Baby Stain, my little Baby Stain. (a beat) Go easy on her, that's all I'm asking of you. Go easy on her. Don't listen to her foul-mouthed ravings; they're just her way of hurting her mother. Her mother was unfair with her, with all of us, to tell the truth, and that flipped her switch, as they say these days. She claims she doesn't want to do anything with her life, at least not anything

that would flatter our pride. But I feel that, with you... You
understand, she just needs to get some fresh air into her mind,
she needs space, someplace bigger to hold everything she refuses
to give to others. Because we're born to love, Ikedia, and to give.
Where will she put all the love she has? (*a beat*) This town has
become too small for her since the events. Unpredictable as raw
freedom, but she's a good girl, you'll see. (*a beat*) She never
leaves the house. Or almost... Once she did run away.
Otherwise... Except to the movies. And then very rarely. Even
her schooling was done at home. She slams her door shut, she
watches TV, she disappears into her books like a novice in
prayer. Or she howls, she locks herself in her room and she
howls, all night long she howls. Like an animal, she howls at
death and God knows what else. She spends days on end without
leaving her room or seeing another face. Howling, reading,
watching television, more howling. That's no life for a young
woman. (*a beat*) You've done her a lot of good. Just your
presence. You've seen it, she laughs now. Finally, she's laughing
again. She runs through the house, she's enjoying herself.

IKEDIA:
Your daughter's belly is full.

FATHER: (*silence*)
I know.

BABY STAIN'S VOICE:
Ikedia! Ikedia!

IKEDIA:
You know everything that goes on here.

FATHER:
That's what this town is like: everybody knows everything about
everybody else. But they act like they don't. When she shot the

mask, the whole town saw her, the whole city heard, but nobody moved a muscle. She said she fired at random. But no choice is ever accidental... even if, from a certain point of view, it was an accident. She could just as well have killed a tourist. She had to do it, that's all.

BABY STAIN'S VOICE:
Ikedia! Ikedia!

FATHER:
Was it your father?

IKEDIA:
Call me Ikedia.

FATHER:
Was it your father?

IKEDIA:
I told you to call me Ikedia.

FATHER:
It was your father.

IKEDIA:
This is the story of a woman... This is the story of a woman who's waiting... This is the story of a woman who's waiting at a window... This is the story of a woman at a window, waiting for her man to return. The man who didn't close the freezer door tight. Which often happens. So the woman, it's inevitable, grumbles about how she works like a dog to find the money to buy food and put it away like it should be put away in the freezer, while other people have nothing better to do than not close the freezer door properly so everything she's worked her fingers to the bone to buy thaws out. She complains. She

complains about everything in general. The man says okay I'm going down to buy cigarettes. That's his way of letting the storm blow over. *(a beat)* Later I looked out the window he was dancing in front of the subway station across from our building. When he needed money for cigarettes he danced in front of the subway entrance. When I looked out the window again he wasn't there and I said to myself he's made enough to buy cigarettes. My mother thought it was because of what she'd said about people who don't close the freezer door tight and let everything thaw that she'd busted her ass buying. Then she sat down. At the window. Where I saw him dance for the last time. She was waiting for him to come back. This is the story of a wife. *(a beat)* The article mentioned a dead mask. Heart attack while he was dancing. The article mentioned a mask without a past so I thought it was him.

FATHER:

Before he came along, we'd never seen anything like that before. He was a man who, how could I put it... He came and went, and he stood in the Square, across from the station, he danced and people threw him a few coins. Always the same music. Always the same dance. Nobody paid him much attention. I couldn't describe him to you myself, and I saw him dance hundreds of times. Actually, now that I think of it, he was invisible. That's the word – invisible. He was there but not there... You see, no one... especially not her. His life was his life. No one ever asked him... You understand, as long as he was willing to dance... and not get mixed up in other people's business, his life was his life. That's the way we are in this place...

IKEDIA:

The article mentioned an eclipse...

FATHER:

Yes. Right after the shot rang out. As if the sun had hidden its face so as not to be a witness...

BABY STAIN'S VOICE:
Ikedia! Ikedia!

FATHER:
We'd better go back. *(picks a poppy)* Why must we be the only ones to pay? From the very start the whole town knew about it. So you'll have to burn it down as well.

IKEDIA:
Of course I will. And if the guilt of the noonday light is proven, I'll burn the sun down too.

FATHER: *(offering him the flower)*
Poppies are the only flowers she can stand in this garden... But of course you must know that. Give it to her. Say it comes from you. It'll make her happy.

Tiny Tears of Wonderment

Inside the house. During the scene, the mask will reappear in the breach in the wall at the rear and will dance as if in slow motion, without music. Only the mother will see it.

BABY STAIN:
Ikedia! Where did my father drag him off to? He must be filling his head up with all kinds of lies.

MOTHER:
Don't be absurd. The truth about you is just as juicy as any lie.

BABY STAIN:
Getting jealous again?

MOTHER:

Stop twitching your backside! Stop it! Tell me what he's got in that bag.

BABY STAIN:

You'll have to ask nicer than that.

MOTHER:

You have no idea... you don't even know.

BABY STAIN:

Of course I do. But that's not what you want to know. What interests you is what he did to me in my room, what parts of my flesh his tongue licked, then returned to lick again...

MOTHER:

Shut up!

BABY STAIN:

You're getting excited, aren't you? All kinds of pictures are tripping over each other in your mind, but I won't tell you because then you'll want to seduce him, just to see... and just to bug me... You couldn't even begin to imagine what Ikedia did to me, so you'd better imagine the worst.

MOTHER:

Don't make such an effort to wallow in the mud. Stop forcing it. Besides what he did to you with his tongue and all the rest, what's he got in that bag?

BABY STAIN:

You're consumed by curiosity and jealousy, aren't you? But that'll just have to be one thing I saw that you'll never see. Because if I told you it would burn your eardrums, if you saw it, it would fry the pupils of your eyes.

MOTHER:
It's the proof, right? The proof.

BABY STAIN:
The proof of what?

MOTHER:
Forget it, forget it...

BABY STAIN:
You want me to tell you?

MOTHER:
Be quiet, I'm thinking. I know he didn't tell you anything. Maybe you did get down on all fours and spread yourself like an anthurium, you still don't know anything...

BABY STAIN:
You're in great form tonight, old lady.

MOTHER:
I'm not your old lady, you slut.

BABY STAIN:
That's how I like you, when your mouth overflows with spiders and rats like an old cesspool.

MOTHER:
Shut up, I'm thinking! He's not Ikedia... doesn't have a cast in his eye... or rainbows either... carries around a bag...

BABY STAIN:
And the things he did to my daughter! Just thinking about them, oh, my God, I'm so ashamed!

MOTHER:

You think you're pretty smart?

BABY STAIN:

He scares you, doesn't he? Admit it – he scares you. Well, you're right to be afraid.

MOTHER:

Whoever he is, his game is going to be up soon enough. I called the police and they'll be here any minute.

BABY STAIN:

You didn't call anybody. You're talking to yourself, as usual. What are you going to tell the cops? That Nosferatu, disguised as a young man, walked through the front door of this house, sunk his teeth into your daughter's breasts, sucked out all her blood, then burned down the place? They'll ask you who did it. "He's right there." "Where?" "There, there, right there!" "But there's nobody there, Ma'am." "That's absurd! – what do you mean, there's nobody?" "There's nobody, Ma'am." Because there won't be anybody, Mama. Ikedia will have flown away. And they'll laugh in your face and you'll feel like an ass. Take it from me, Ikedia's my thing. Who opened the door for him? Who told you his name was Ikedia? Who? Ikedia is the wind I blow through your empty heads. Nothing but wind! And why did this young man set fire to your house, Ma'am? Go ahead, you tell me! But you don't want people doubting the last few grains of sanity you have left. Take Papa. He's looking on the bright side. He's giving him a guided tour of the house, the bathroom, the laundry room, the kitchen, the library, the basement, the garden. He's sitting tight till things blow over. But they won't blow over. In the end this house will be reduced to ashes.

MOTHER:

Stop puffing yourself up. This time it's not about you. This time you're not centre stage.

BABY STAIN:

Whose story do you think this is?
Ikedia
is my thing, I'm telling you.
I invented him,
chip of bone by chip of bone,
slice of flesh by slice of flesh
drop of blood by drop of blood.
Then I blew a starburst of soul into him.
That's what I created, Mama,
to give you the slap of your life.
Ikedia is me, he's my story.

MOTHER:

So tell me what he has in that bag!

BABY STAIN:

Nothing that would pierce your eardrums or burn your eyes.
You're right, I have no idea. I don't know what he's carrying
around in that goddamn bag of his and I don't care. But when I
think that the fire that will burn down this house will be
gratuitous, I get itchy between my legs.

MOTHER:

Then scratch it!

BABY STAIN:

No, not right now. I won't scratch my itch. I'll let my impatience
build while I go on creating Ikedia. Step by step. Without
knowing what he'll end up doing. Because I'm working in the
dark. Any moment, he could balk like a horse in front of a jump,
that's possible. Then I'll have to figure out the next step like a
blind guide. Let my impatience slip in and out, between my
thighs. Slowly. Taking my time. I have all night. All I need is to
make him put one foot in front of the other, carefully, one-two,

one-two, one-two, one-two, one-two, one-two, one-two... until the final explosion. And then, only then, will I scratch the itch between my legs, delicately, with my fingertips, and let my sex sob with delight, let it stream with tiny warm tears, delicate tears of wonderment at this gratuitous act.

The Garden

Ikedia and the father cross the living room, laughing uproariously.

IKEDIA:
  Wait, wait, that's not all! So the lady looks at the gentleman with this incredulous, half-opened mouth and stammers, "Is that so?"

They laugh harder as the two women look on, astonished.

The men cross the stage without paying them any attention, completely absorbed in their laughter.

MOTHER: *(seeing the gun in her husband's hand)*
  What are you doing with that gun?

FATHER:
  It's Ikedia's... "Is that so?"

The two men dissolve in giggles.

MOTHER: *(the father hands her the gun like a child caught in the act)*
  Are you all right?

FATHER:
  Why wouldn't I be?

Ikedia gives the poppy to Baby Stain.

BABY STAIN:
   For me?

She kisses him.

MOTHER: *(to her daughter)*
   Go put the turkey in the oven!

FATHER: *(with childish enthusiasm)*
   Don't bother. Not this time. Ikedia says...

MOTHER:
   Ikedia says what?

FATHER: *(hiding a laugh)*
   Ikedia says... Tell her yourself, Ikedia.

IKEDIA:
   It's shit.

FATHER:
   That's it, it's shit... He means it's stupid.

MOTHER:
   What's stupid?

BABY STAIN:
   It's stupid, stupid!

IKEDIA:
   Turkey on a day like this is stupid.

MOTHER:
   You'll need to change clothes for supper, Ikedia.

FATHER:
So no turkey...

BABY STAIN:
Papa will lend you something, right?

MOTHER:
No turkey tonight because that's what Ikedia says?

IKEDIA:
No. Because it's shit.

BABY STAIN:
He'd look nice in your flannel suit, Papa...

MOTHER:
So what do we do, Ikedia?

IKEDIA:
Nothing. We improvise.

BABY STAIN: *(busy at Ikedia's feet)*
What size do you wear?

MOTHER:
Ah! We improvise...

BABY STAIN: *(taking off one of Ikedia's shoes)*
Let's see if you wear the same size as Papa.

FATHER:
Because... Ikedia, can I say it for you? Because a holiday isn't a
retrospective, it's not a summing up... Is that it? It's a time... stop
me if I'm misinterpreting you, Ikedia. *(reciting)*
It's a time to shed,

the way snakes do,
the time we slough off
our wilted old lives
a time when promises of life
begin to bud anew...

BABY STAIN:
I always knew you were full of words.

FATHER:
I think that's very interesting, very, very interesting... Intellectually very stimulating... And then there's this: (*imitating a surprised woman*) "Is that so?" (*both break out laughing again*) So come on, follow me!

IKEDIA:
Everybody into the garden. That's where the celebration will take place this year, in the belly of the earth, with the starry sky looking on.

MOTHER:
Who's making the decisions here?

BABY STAIN:
Ikedia is deciding tonight because he's my guest.

FATHER:
The garden? Well, why not? The garden is an excellent place for that. Strange we never thought of it before. The weather is magnificent, the sky is clear and the moon is full. It's perfect. There's no other word for it: perfect.

MOTHER:
Perfect, perfect, but have you thought of my coelogynes... my lycastes... my laelias... my lady's slippers... If you knew how much trouble it was to convince my lady's slippers to bloom!

Those plants are very fragile, you understand, very beautiful but very fragile like all beautiful things...

IKEDIA:
No harm will come to your orchids, Madam...

MOTHER:
He knows they're orchids, dear!

IKEDIA:
I love orchids.

MOTHER:
Dear, he loves orchids!

FATHER:
He amazes me, he astonishes me, he delights me!

MOTHER:
Now, I'm reassured... Truly reassured, You can't be such a bad man after all. As for my daughter – a disaster! She has no taste... no sensitivity...

BABY STAIN:
I don't like plants that you grow and don't eat.

MOTHER:
So much for flowers... As far as I know, no one's soul was ever uplifted by eating carrots! I gave her a nice little pot of browallias to spruce up her window, and go with the Chinese jasmine... I'm sure you saw, there's Chinese jasmine around her window... Don't you think it was a good idea, Ikedia, browallias in a shower of Chinese jasmine?

IKEDIA:
Magnificent.

MOTHER:

Well, Ikedia, you might not believe me but it's the truth. The
honest truth. The next morning, when I went by her window...
My God, the horror! The carnage! The mere thought of it makes
me shiver... A complete genocide! And I'm being careful not to
exaggerate... The heads of the browallias were lying in the dust,
beneath her window... Heads that had been cut off! That girl had
massacred them, one by one. Methodically. The frail little white
throats of the browallias – sliced open! Can you imagine
anything more savage, Ikedia? The fierce barbaric impulse that
chokes that girl's soul is positively frightening. Frightening.
When I think that thing came out of me! Thank God, I only had
one. No taste, no sensitivity for... Actually, yes. For poppies. Her
sensitivity stops at poppies! Of course, poppies... poppies. Isn't it
true, dear, you adore poppies? (*Baby Stain doesn't answer*) I'm the
only one in this house who looks after those poor plants...
Fortunately, you... Anyway, now you understand, Ikedia, why it
isn't possible to hold the celebration in the garden.

IKEDIA:

But I'm telling you that not a single one of your flowers will
have its throat slashed, and that we're holding the celebration in
the garden.

MOTHER:

But, Ikedia, you, such a charming, sensitive young man... And
besides... This is my house!

BABY STAIN:

It's my house too, and he's my guest.

MOTHER:

The answer is no, I'm telling you!

IKEDIA:

I'm telling you it's yes.

MOTHER:

Ikedia, don't listen to her... Let's talk like sane, sensible people. Right, Ikedia, like people endowed with sensitivity and discernment. Consider the flowers a moment, consider their suffering... And besides, what about the neighbours... There's always the neighbours... The noise and the... No, no, no, I won't have it.

IKEDIA:

You have no neighbours. Your house is isolated.

MOTHER:

I see you haven't been wasting your time... Underneath it all, you're just like her. But you won't be talking so big when the police show up. I won't let the first criminal who walks in here tell me where I'm going to have my holiday supper. I've called them, you know.

IKEDIA:

You didn't call anyone. The phone line's been cut.

FATHER:

But... Ikedia, you must be joking...

Radiant, Baby Stain throws her arms around Ikedia and kisses him.

BABY STAIN:

So it's really true, you weren't just showing off. You really are going to reduce this house to ashes.

IKEDIA:

You'll just have to learn to live with the idea. Tonight, use your imagination and celebrate like there's no tomorrow. *(to the father)* Lead on!

BABY STAIN:
Finally this ship has a captain.

Ikedia and the father cross the stage.
The mother points the gun at them as they disappear.

BABY STAIN:
Would you really have shot them?

MOTHER:
They're just kids. Men are just kids. When two of them get together, the nonsense starts.

BABY STAIN:
I'd watch out if I were you, Mama. Ikedia is stealing Papa from you.

MOTHER:
You don't know anything about men. He's the one who's stealing Ikedia from you

Ritual

The garden.

A movie screen has been set up, perhaps a large TV screen. Baby Stain is sitting on the red couch. Ikedia and the father have their backs turned to the mother, who is pointing the gun at them, as if she hadn't moved from the previous scene.

BABY STAIN: *(detached)*
The last time you touched a gun, a man died in this town.

Baby Stain's words set off the mother's attack. The mother drops the gun and begins feverishly looking for her pills. In vain. Finally she collapses in pain.

IKEDIA: *(holding up the bottle of pills)*
I have them.

MOTHER:
Give them to me!

BABY STAIN:
Ask nicer.

MOTHER:
Throw them to me!

BABY STAIN:
Don't you do it, Ikedia. Even if she grovels at your feet, make her ask nicely.

FATHER:
You know she won't do that.

BABY STAIN:
Make her beg for pardon!

FATHER:
For what?

BABY STAIN:
For everything. Have I ever pointed a pistol at one of your guests? Make her beg your forgiveness! I've never invited anyone into this house, and the first guest I have, she wants to kill him! Make her beg!

FATHER:

Every second counts, Ikedia. She's going to die.

BABY STAIN:

That's crap! Evil has a heart of steel. I want to see her crawl and beg for forgiveness.

FATHER:

She'll never do it.

BABY STAIN:

Then she can croak with her lips sealed!

The father tries to take the pills from Ikedia. Ikedia pushes him away; he falls to the ground as the pills go flying. The father gathers up a few of them and gives them to his wife.

FATHER:

Whatever your reasons...

BABY STAIN:

He doesn't have any. He was passing by he saw the light he said to himself why don't I burn down that house? That's it.

FATHER:

My wife did act... I grant you that in other circumstances...

IKEDIA:

But it was just for fun.

FATHER:

For fun?

IKEDIA:

Yeah, sure, for fun, I was just joking... fooling around.

FATHER:

For fun... You see, Ikedia, a family is like a body... yes, this body, yours, for example, with its skin, nerves, veins, organs, red blood cells, white blood cells, antibodies... A body is a world, a kingdom. And when a foreigner penetrates it, unexpectedly – I would like to stress that – unexpectedly...

BABY STAIN:

Stop bugging him! He said it was just a joke.

IKEDIA:

No, really, it's true, it was just a joke. Sincerely.

FATHER:

... you can't just walk in off the street, you can't just do whatever you feel like, and walk away when the feeling strikes you. The white blood cells and antibodies act as sentinels, if you like, guards. They're the watchdogs. They approach the foreign body, circle it, sniff it, the way dogs do... And whatever you do, don't insult me by thinking I'm trying to reduce you to the state of some vulgar bacterium, some virus, Ikedia, spare me your suspicions...

BABY STAIN:

You can sure be a pain when you get going, Papa!

IKEDIA:

If you can't make any jokes around here, then...

FATHER:

No, let me finish! My wife is the guardian of this house, of this kingdom, and she has always taken it upon herself to preserve its integrity. Like a watchdog. Like a priestess... Now I'm not trying to excuse her, she did point a gun at you... But, Ikedia, remember the foreign body –

BABY STAIN:

He's not a foreign body, he's my guest!

FATHER:

A guest...

BABY STAIN:

He's my man!

FATHER:

As a guest, Ikedia, did you show yourself worthy of our hospitality?

IKEDIA:

I have no idea what you're talking about. No idea at all. If you ask me, you've got no sense of humour. Do you really think I would have let your wife croak? Really, who do you think I am? It was just a game. Just for fun. I had the rubber band of her life in my hand and I was pulling on it, pulling as far as I could until the very last second... the way you hold a friend's head under water to feel that moment when he begins to fight for air... and then, one breath from the end, just when the rubber band is about to snap – bang! you toss her the pills. It's that simple.

BABY STAIN:

When you do it right, it can really be a lot of fun.

IKEDIA:

You disappoint me. Baby Stain has a better sense of humour than you do.

BABY STAIN:

You heard him, didn't you? He didn't come here to hurt anyone.

MOTHER:

What did you call her? *(silence)* Her, yes, her, what did you call her?

IKEDIA:

Baby Stain.

MOTHER:

Ah!

FATHER:

I had begged you for just one thing...

MOTHER:

I don't want you begging! Stop grovelling! I'm the one who's supposed to get down on her knees and beg for pardon. *(she falls to her knees)* Well, here I am, both knees in the dust, here I am, kneeling, not to beg for forgiveness, oh no, I have nothing to be forgiven for. On the contrary: I'm the one who's owed reparations. I'm on my knees asking for someone to tell me why. Why have you singled out my family? The happiness we enjoy, myself and my loved ones, we didn't steal it. I work hard, my husband works hard. We make money, a lot of money. But we contribute regularly to charitable causes. Doctors Without Borders. CARE. The Red Cross, baby seals, the Salvation Army, street kids, the Lepers' Foundation, the Association for the Blind, the Little Brothers of the Hungry, the women of Afghanistan, Chinese girl orphans... We give to all of them. Why have you singled us out? Our family ties are as solid as any in this city. We have three televisions, one in the living room, one in our room and another in our daughter's room...

BABY STAIN:

I'm not part of your crap!

MOTHER:

... My husband plays golf, oh, not as well as he'd like to, but he'll improve his game, he has the perseverance for it. The mortgage is entirely paid off, the Blue Cross, the life insurance, the retirement plans. Why have you singled us out? The happiness we enjoy, myself and my family, we didn't steal it. I work hard, my husband works hard. We make money, a lot of money. But we contribute regularly to charitable causes...

BABY STAIN:

You said that already, Mama.

MOTHER:

You shut up! Shut your trap! You heard me. I said shut your trap, you piece of filth! You're the one who's always brought shame into this house. If it weren't for you, this shitty little...

FATHER:

No, dear!

MOTHER:

Shut up, I said! If it weren't for you, this shitty little fart wouldn't have slithered into this house. *(Ikedia whispers something in the father's ear)* The three of us were enjoying ourselves, the evening was going along just fine...

FATHER:

Dear?

MOTHER:

What is it?

FATHER:

Ikedia says that...

MOTHER:
Ikedia says what?

FATHER:
Ikedia says that... Interrupt me if I'm... Ikedia says that your mouth is working faster than your brain.

MOTHER:
Oh, really?

FATHER:
Also, he's asking you... (*Ikedia whispers something to him*) Yes! Ikedia demands that you take back the word "shitty."

MOTHER:
Oh, yeah? And how come?

FATHER: (*Ikedia whispers*)
Because he could get very unpleasant.

MOTHER:
Really? I'll do better than that. Not only is he a shitty little fart, he's a pathetic asshole.

BABY STAIN:
Mother!

MOTHER:
You shut up! (*to her husband*) Tell him he doesn't scare me! You don't scare me! You're a fool who got pussy-whipped by some girl who's still wet behind the ears! You don't scare me! "I'm going to burn down this house!" My ass you're going to burn down this house! You and your sack of clichés! You don't scare me! Now what's Ikedia saying?

FATHER:

Ikedia is begging me to hold him back, otherwise he won't be responsible for his actions.

MOTHER:

Go ahead, don't be responsible (*opens her blouse*), here's my breast, open your bag, take out your weapon and wound it. Go ahead, go ahead, do it! (*she rubs up against Ikedia, who doesn't know what to do*) You want to shock the middle class? You want to scare them? You're completely behind the times! Anyway, you're finished now, asshole! Don't you realize that girl's got you by the short hairs? Come on, make a move, you little jerk-off!

IKEDIA:

That's not true! That's not true! I never jerk off!

MOTHER:

Little jerk-off! Little jerk-off! Little jerk-off!

IKEDIA:

I've never jerked off in my life!

MOTHER:

You're the biggest jerk-off going! If you were a man, a real one, with balls and a cock to match, you'd take on a real woman, not a girl. Jerk-off!

IKEDIA:

You asked for it.

He takes out his gun.

MOTHER:

Oh, shit, the little asshole's got a gun!

IKEDIA:

I'm going to waste you, you old bitch!

FATHER:

Get a hold of yourself, Ikedia!

BABY STAIN:

Let them work it out. Did you hear the way she treated him?

IKEDIA:

I'm not a little jerk-off! And I'm going to whack you, you old hag!

A shot rings out.

MOTHER:

You've lost it, Ikedia. I was just joking... just having some fun...
fooling around.

IKEDIA:

Shut your mouth! You called me a little jerk-off and I never
jerk off!

MOTHER:

Okay, Ikedia, I take it back, I was wrong. You're not a jerk-off.

IKEDIA:

Too late. I'm going to smear you all over the place!

He runs after the mother. They both disappear into the wings.

FATHER:

They're in the laundry room.

BABY STAIN:
No, they're in the kitchen. Listen.

Sounds of pots and pans.

FATHER:
You're right, they're in the kitchen. *(silence suddenly reigns)* Baby Stain...

BABY STAIN:
No, Papa.

FATHER:
My sweet Baby Stain...

BABY STAIN:
Be reasonable, Papa.

A shot is heard.

FATHER:
Shit! *(silence)* You think he killed her?

BABY STAIN:
Here's hoping.

FATHER:
You knew he was armed?

BABY STAIN:
Everyone is armed these days, Papa.

More noise of pots and pans.

FATHER:
I think your mother's still on her feet.

Another shot.

BABY STAIN:
He's finished her off!

FATHER:
You think so?

BABY STAIN:
Listen!

The mother moans long and hard.

FATHER:
We are but a shadow on the grass!

BABY STAIN:
Well, she did go looking for trouble.

FATHER:
The best ones always die first.

BABY STAIN:
There were extenuating circumstances.

Another shot.

FATHER:
He's emptying the whole chamber into her!

BABY STAIN:
It's obvious she didn't call you a jerk-off.

Music comes up. Something like a Strauss waltz. Ikedia and the mother enter dancing.

FATHER:
Are you okay, dear?

MOTHER:
Open your eyes and see.

BABY STAIN:
Happy now?

MOTHER:
It's not what you think.

BABY STAIN:
I don't think. I observe.

IKEDIA:
Your mother is right...

BABY STAIN:
I don't want to hear another word out of you!

MOTHER:
Sting me again, Ikedia!

The music picks up. The mother leads Ikedia onto the floor. They turn like whirling dervishes. They dance faster and faster and the mother laughs harder and harder. Then, abruptly, the music stops. Ikedia leaves the mother alone in the middle of the dance floor. She staggers, then collapses heavily, overcome by dizziness. Her laughter is both compulsive and joyful.

MOTHER:

Ikedia! Ikedia makes a woman happy... And I'm happy... Ikedia makes a woman happy... Ikedia, my sweet... We're so much alike... It's absurd how much alike we are... I could show up, like you... like you... from nowhere, like you, Ikedia... show up in the night... with a vengeful fist, and burn down anything I want to. Because you, Ikedia, you have a secret mission, right? A secret, terrible mission for everyone in this town. Not because the city is guilty of some blasphemy, oh no, people like you and me, Ikedia, our secrets aren't that rational. One person, just one. One act of evil is enough to burn down the world. That's something I learned... In a book that girl gave me... If you only knew the crap she reads!

BABY STAIN:

Mama!

MOTHER:

... A man, as gentle as a lamb, but angry, was going to bomb a Mercedes... or was it a limousine... Another man, a real ogre, was in the Mercedes... An incredibly wicked, perverse individual... Imagine, Ikedia, this monster made it his business to sit between his two children, in the back seat of the Mercedes... Between two children. So the lamb refuses to throw the bomb that will blow up the limousine... or was it a Mercedes... because of the innocent children. Well, I would have set off the bomb, children or no children. Even if I had to step over the corpses of nine hundred and ninety-nine little innocents to murder the villain, I wouldn't hesitate. And I know you would have done the same thing, Ikedia. Because the evil that a single man can inflict on the beauty and innocence of the world is always greater, profoundly and durably greater, than the good that a thousand innocents might accomplish. It's absurd but that's the way it is. So I would have come out of nowhere, with a vengeful fist, and set fire to the city. But you won't put the torch to this house, Ikedia.

Because of the flowers. In the name of the flowers. Because they are the prayer of the world. Look! Look around... Every day I put everything that Eden can offer into this garden. You don't burn down paradise, Ikedia, you eat its forbidden fruit... In this city, there are individuals so hateful, so terribly hateful that I often wish for their death, even if it means an apocalypse that would wipe us all out... Tell you what – tomorrow, at daybreak, I'll point them out to you and you can burn them. And if the city objects you can burn it too... But not the flowers...

IKEDIA:

Tell your wife to shut her trap!

MOTHER:

... I'll testify on your behalf... I have connections... You'll see, Ikedia, my sweet, I know how to handle people... But not the flowers... And if all the police in the world come after you and track you down in the red dust of Arizona... you know Arizona, Ikedia? Arizona... Where the Indians live... where the Hopi Indians are... I'll hide you in the belly of Arizona's extinct volcanoes...

BABY STAIN:

Mama, can't you see how ridiculous you are?

MOTHER:

My sugar sweet... And here I'd resigned myself to you burning down the house.

IKEDIA:

But I will burn it down. When a helicopter lands, the pilot chooses a spot to set down the craft. A gust of wind might push the helicopter to the right or the left, but the pilot never takes his eyes off that spot. Whatever happens, he'll always bring it in at the chosen place. When I have an idea, I stick to it.

MOTHER:
Now, now, now... Just keep being a sweetheart, will you?

IKEDIA:
Fine. Let's start where we left off.

FATHER:
This boy impresses me. I'm telling you, he really impresses me. He really does...

The Kiss

The father and mother act in concert.
Ikedia carefully reloads his revolver. Baby Stain's eyes are glued to him.

MOTHER:
May I ask you... Now that we're on good terms, now that we're more than just friends... can I ask you a favour, Ikedia, my little sugar? Just one favour...

BABY STAIN:
In exchange for what?

MOTHER:
I have nothing against improvising, Ikedia. In fact I'm beginning to think that my husband and I don't improvise enough. I'm beginning to think so. From now on we'll be improvising more often, I'll see to it, you can be sure. Because, you understand –

BABY STAIN:
What about your favour, Mama?

MOTHER:

Oh, yes, of course. It's a kiss. My husband and I met in a movie house. You understand, when you're young, you go out to the movies... We kissed for the first time to this kiss. The first time at the movies.

FATHER:

We didn't know each other, we hadn't even met...

MOTHER:

... but during this kiss his lips found their way to my lips...

FATHER:

... and my lips found their way to hers.

MOTHER:

So, you understand, Ikedia, every year, over the holidays, we show the kiss, and it brings us back to years past, when my husband was still full of pep...

FATHER:

... when... whether it was in the laundry room, the kitchen, the basement or the attic, we spent most of our time...

MOTHER:

You understand? Improvising, as you put it so nicely... improvising.

FATHER:

This little ritual is so important to my wife. It's the only time we step out of line...

BABY STAIN:

Granted.

The image of an endless kiss taken from Gone with the Wind *– or some similar film – is projected on the screen. It's the image that the father was vainly trying to focus on at the beginning of the play.*

FATHER:
Doesn't the condemned man have the right to a last cigarette, Ikedia?

BABY STAIN:
I said, granted!

MOTHER:
So you agree, Ikedia?

BABY STAIN: *(pointing at the screen)*
What's that?

FATHER:
Look, dear, it's you and me.

Silence. The father and mother gaze at the kiss. The image repeats and they never tire of it. Baby Stain still hasn't taken her eyes off Ikedia who is busy caressing his revolver.

MOTHER: *(obviously excited by the kiss)*
Dear, I feel like powdering my nose. Want to come along?

They exit.

You Will Love Me

The kiss continues to occupy the screen. Ikedia silently strokes his weapon with the grandiloquent style of a gangster in a B-grade movie.

BABY STAIN:

You have nothing to say? You don't think I deserve a little explanation? *(silence)* Not a word? You don't give a damn about what I might feel? *(silence)* All right. I just hope you haven't forgotten there's a fire waiting for you... Sure, you've already lit my mother's ass on fire. *(silence)* What a fool I am! When I think I loved you from the first day I packed my bags. I loved you without knowing you. I loved you even though you're not Ikedia. What a fool I am! A fool! A fool! *(silence)* Nothing to say? *(silence)* You can't even say you're sorry? *(silence)* Actually you don't love me. Not yet. But you will, Ikedia.

Believe me, you will love me.
I can be patient.
I will teach you to love me
the way I would train an animal.
You will love me
and you will love loving me.
I will make you my addict,
my addict, my addict, my addict,
and you will beg for more.
I will keep you from laying eyes
on other women,
and you will love it.
Your body won't awaken
for any other body but mine,
and you will love it.
I will hurt you,
as much as possible,
the way you can hurt

only those you love,
and you will love it.
You will see what kind of fly-trap
my love can be;
you will be the fly
and you will be grateful to me.
You will love me with a sleep-walker's love.
You will see,
I have the patience of a saint,
and you will love me.

IKEDIA:
  Baby Stain.

BABY STAIN:
  Don't touch me. You still have that woman's filth on you...

IKEDIA:
  Baby Stain.

BABY STAIN:
  No, don't sully me. We're running out of time, so do what you've
  come here to do. If you really have something to do... Think of
  the man you've come here for and do it. But do it quick, Ikedia,
  time's wasting and we have to be gone by daybreak.

IKEDIA:
  Close your eyes.

  She closes her eyes.

  *Ikedia opens his bag; intense light flows from it. From the bag he
  takes out human bones and lays them down in a circle. Then he
  takes a mask out of the bag and puts it on.*

  Baby Stain opens her eyes.

Ikedia dances the dance of the mask previously danced by the father.
Upon the first steps and the first notes, the mother and father come
rushing in. They are completely naked but don't seem to realize it;
they are too absorbed by Ikedia's dance.

IKEDIA:
    Alo alo
    Se mwen mas aganman
    Se mwen premye pitit lakreyasyon
    Lè lemonn ta pral koumanse
    Lè m te fenk fèt
    Patanko gen anyen
    Ni pip ni tabak
    Latè pat latè sou batistè latè
    Nan vid premye tan yo ki te san bout
    Latè te ou moso vyann nan vant manman l
    Po li te si tèlman fen
    Pou me te mache
    Se fwole m te fwole-l pou m pa chire po l
    Konsa konsa depi lè sa a
    M mache kanyank kanyank
    Alo alo
    Se mwen mas krapo
    Se mwen premye pitit lakreyasyon
    Lè lemonn ta pral koumanse
    Lè m te fenk fèt
    Patanko gen anyen
    Ni pip ni tabak
    Latè pat latè sou batistè latè
    Nan vid premye tan yo ki te san bout
    Kèk zetwal tap flote
    Pou pouse do m
    M te sote pasi pala
    Konsa konsa depi lè sa a
    Mache m se te ponpe tik tik

Alo alo
Se mwen mas gwo zwazo bèk fè
Lè lemonn ta pral koumanse
Lè m te fenk fèt
Patanko gen anyen
Ni pip ni tabak
Latè pat latè sou batistè latè
Nan vid premye tan yo ki te san bout
An grenn senk m tap flote
Lè manman m kraze rak
San yon bout vyann latè
San menm yon moso tè
M te fann nenm
Pou m te entere manman m
Konsa depi lè sa a
Nen m tankou yon tonm ki plante nan figi m.

He dances to the point of exhaustion, then collapses.

BABY STAIN: *(to her mother)*
Now you know the reason, so learn to live with it. Now you
know why, so go ahead! Do it, do it!

IKEDIA:
Three days ago I climbed to the top of the hill that you –

FATHER:
The dog cemetery.

MOTHER:
We were so comfortable. Just the three of us. The evening
promised to be just fine... First the glass of Condrieu. My
husband adores Condrieu wines. Then the meal. In silence. Like
a prayer. Then, over cognac, we would have looked back over
the year. Until midnight. Midnight means champagne. We would

have risen from the table. Lifted our glasses. The three of us. To wish each other happy new year. With an embrace. In total silence. As if we were praying. Then there would have been the telephone calls. Family. Friends. We would have called too. Telephone calls. Then that girl would have gone up to her room, and just the two of us, we would have settled in the warmth of an embrace in the armchair. To watch it. One more time. Our kiss... our kiss... I'm Viven Leigh, and my husband is Clark Gable...

IKEDIA:

... There, on the bare stone, in the midst of the putrefying flesh of dogs...

MOTHER:

Oh, Ikedia, my sugar sweet, what are you doing in the middle of that graveyard?

She takes a step towards the circle of bones.

IKEDIA:

Don't come in here!

BABY STAIN:

Didn't you hear? "Don't come in here!"

Without roughness, she pushes her mother away from the circle, repeating "Don't come in here!" Her frightened mother runs off, pursued by Baby Stain's repeated "Don't come in here!" Both women wheel around the circle.

MOTHER:

What does this girl have against me? Why her? Her.

IKEDIA:

There, on the bare stone... there, in the midst of the putrefying flesh of dogs, a man's face, his eyes turned to the sun –

BABY STAIN:

Now the reason is clear, so try to live with it!

FATHER:

It's the law... the law here... After seven days if no one comes to claim the body... That's the law... the law is for everyone...

MOTHER:

Maybe because he didn't fit in here... I aim I fire he crumples in slow motion... I hate things that don't fit in... Because I suppose my husband told you I fired at random... I aim I fire he crumples... It's absurd... When the car sped across the Square... I fire... The car sped across the Square then... She's sitting next to me... The car speeding across the Square... He crumples in slow motion... The car circles the Square, again and again. I watch... In slow motion... I watch for the look she caresses her father with...

BABY STAIN:

But I was only seven years old! You're crazy, you've always been crazy!

MOTHER:

He's her father and she caresses him with her eyes, she's his daughter and he excites her with his music: my little Baby Stain. I always hoped he'd croon that delicious blasphemy to me too: Baby Stain... The car careens across the Square... I aim and I fire... I didn't see him till afterwards. First the imbecilic herd of tourists. Then him... In slow motion he crumples... He's there, in the middle of them, as usual he's dancing. Even when the city is sleeping, and the Square is deserted, when it's raining and windy, he's still dancing, he's always dancing... I aim and I fire –

BABY STAIN:

That's just talk! Empty words! Watch out, Ikedia, keep your guard up. Don't trust her, she's trying to corrupt you with the bile of her pity. Keep your guard up, Ikedia. Dance and dodge. Keep both fists up and counterpunch. When you waved that gun and forced me to get in the car, you didn't know where you were going or what you would do. Only one thing counted: to put the fear of God into me. The car is on the Square, you roll down the window and yell: "Look what your mother can do when you push her too far!" You have the gun between your legs. The car slows down. I'm sitting next to you, frozen with fear. You grab the gun from between your legs; the whole city sees. You fire; the whole city hears. The mask collapses you turn to me and say, "Now you know how far my madness can go when someone tries to steal what's mine." So stop your bullshit: you would have killed anyone as long as I felt the lead in my own brain... You wanted to put on a real show for me. But you ended up spilling his father's blood.

IKEDIA: (showing the father a hole in the mask)
Doctor, there's a hole here. A bullet hole.

FATHER:

I admit at the time... probably because of the confusion... You see, Ikedia, this is a peaceful little city and people are used to nothing happening... Admittedly, to conclude it was a heart attack... But consider the times! True, there was blood in the hair... But then again! You know what coincidence can do! I didn't see the hole in his head! The blood in his hair, yes, but the hole in his skull, no. You can't imagine how... You can trust my experience as a doctor, it's practically impossible to recover a bullet from that kind of head... And even if I had seen it... how can I put it... the papers, the radio, the television... People were much too quick to make connections, unwarranted relationships, the city was thrown like a sacrificial victim to... No, it would have been too much for such a peaceful city. *(a pause)* Good God! How could I have known? It's not easy to find a bullet in hair like that!

MOTHER:
You have broken into this house, I repeat, broken in through illegal entry, you have spoiled the party, our daughter has opened every fold of her body to you...

BABY STAIN:
Speak for yourself!

MOTHER:
Because... Because one day, Ikedia, my little sugar, I saw him... He'd finished dancing and he was sitting in the café next to the butcher shop that sends out its fumes of pestilence and death under a hot sun. He lifted his mask just enough to take a swallow of beer, and what I saw... just the fraction of a second but I saw it. Nothingness. A face without wrinkles or eyelashes or eyebrows or cheekbones. Nothing at all. Neither disappointment nor the promise of life. Nothing. A face without a face that had frozen into a mask. Nothing. Now you've come in here and conquered this house like a girl whose favours are carelessly offered. I've watched you strut up and down in your greasy jeans like a villain in a Hollywood movie. And I've seen nothing in you, Ikedia, sugar sweet, that reminds me of what I saw in that absence of a face when he lifted his mask to wet his lips with beer. *(silence)* Maybe you do need a father, Ikedia, sugar sweet, but –

BABY STAIN:
Stop calling him that! Stop it! Move, Ikedia, move! Keep your head down! Dance and dodge but don't back down, put up your fists and counterpunch. Move, Ikedia, move! Please, make a move... That's his father's mask, those are his father's bones, that's

his father. You say you shot him by accident? Then he'll be his father by accident. Ikedia, do what you have to and let's get out of here.

MOTHER:

You'll never be more than a war trophy to him.

Baby Stain slaps her mother. Immediately her father leaps at her.

IKEDIA:

Don't touch her!

FATHER:

But how... How could you think I would hit her? What makes you think...

IKEDIA:

Nobody makes me think anything.

FATHER·

But... Ikedia!

Composition

MOTHER: (*Talking to herself after Baby Stain's slap. Uninterrupted words, like background music.*) Stain... stain... stain... Through her, always through her shame has entered this house...
Stain... stain...
Stain... Guilty? Guilty. Guilty for everyone, guilty for the whole city. For a whole life. Guilt without remission. No one can steal my guilt from me. And no one can know its madness.

A beat.

Do you realize, Ikedia, my sugar sweet? Her father she caresses with her eyes, his daughter he excites with his music: Sweet Little Baby Stain. More than once hoped for that song, for me too that delicious blasphemy: Baby Stain...

A beat

Police better call the police the cops too and the firemen. Better call the firemen first.

A beat

Didn't see him till after. First the imbecilic herd of tourists. Then him. There in their midst, like always, dancing. Enough to think when city sleeps,

Square empty, rain, wind, still dancing, always. See him flying flying flying his endless dance in the luminous dust of noon.

Ikedia methodically packs up the bones. The father tries to help him but Ikedia waves him off; he'll do it alone.

BABY STAIN:
She's lost her mind. Let's get out of here.

IKEDIA:
Your suitcase.

BABY STAIN:
No. I'm not taking anything with me.

Ikedia moves off.

BABY STAIN:
You're not forgetting anything, Ikedia?

IKEDIA:
Let's get out of here.

BABY STAIN:
The fire!

IKEDIA:
Are you coming or not?

A beat

Stain... stain... stain... Yes yes call them better call them. But first the firemen.
(Silence)

BABY STAIN:
The fire!

IKEDIA:
No!

BABY STAIN:
The fire!

IKEDIA:
I said no! I found what I was looking for; I heard what I came to hear. Look at them, see the despair they're in.

BABY STAIN:
If you leave this house without...

IKEDIA:
I saw what I wanted to see and I heard what I wanted to hear. *(silence)* Now I leave them to you.

BABY STAIN:
If you only knew the itch I have to burn down this place! But you'll never be healed and you'll always hold it against me. You'll never know peace until you've reduced this house to ashes. A week, a month, a year, a century later you'll

return to set the fire
and seal the pact
with your father. But
when I leave I don't
come back, Ikedia. I
step into the void...
Don't believe what
you see. You see
them naked and
afflicted, ready to
beat their breasts, but
their affliction is just
a miserable
performance. I know
them, they're my
parents, the only
thing they
understand is fire.
No one knows them
better than me,
Ikedia. Fire is the
only way to gain
their respect.

FATHER: (his voice
rising up as from
afar)
... On the banks of
the Euphrates, from
the left bank to the
right rode the bloody
legend of a terrible
warrior named Hajik.
Hajik's glory was
raiding, raping,

spilling blood. Hajik
didn't conquer to
keep, but only to
burn. Only to burn.

MOTHER:
In those days,
Babylon was burying
Nebuchadnezzar.

FATHER:
In those days,
Babylon was burying
Nebuchadnezzar.

FATHER:
Hajik and his armies
laid siege to the
proud and prosperous
city of Ourgashi,
known to be
impenetrable. Hajik
swore he would take
it. The siege lasted
twelve moons. For
twelve moons of
resistance, Ourgashi
was cut off from all
Mesopotamia.
Ourgashi lived by
itself, for itself, for
twelve moons.

MOTHER:
In those days,
Babylon was burying
Nebuchadnezzar.

FATHER:
In those days,
Babylon was burying
Nebuchadnezzar.

FATHER:
One morning of the
thirteenth moon,
along the ramparts of
Ourgashi the proud,
the first signs of
surrender stirred,
then the gates of the
city flew open and
the bridges were
lowered. A clamour
of victory rose up
from Hajik's armies,
drunk with blood-
lust. The legend says
that their voices
could be heard all
the way to the
shadows of the date
palms on the banks
of the Nile. At that
moment, the world
held its breath.
Ourgashi,
defenceless, open,
was offered up to
Hajik's men.

In those days,
Babylon was burying
Nebuchadnezzar.

MOTHER:
In those days,
Babylon was burying
Nebuchadnezzar.

FATHER:
Followed by his men,
Hajik entered
Ourgashi. He
surveyed the city,
and then, to
everyone's
wonderment, he

MOTHER:
In those days,
Babylon was burying
Nebuchadnezzar.

BABY STAIN:
No roof torched, not
a drop of blood
spilled. The city
stood in silent
disbelief. For the
longest time, it
wondered why Hajik
had spared it, why
Hajik had turned his
back on his own
legend.

In those days,
Babylon was burying
Nebuchadnezzar.

BABY STAIN:
For hours, Ourgashi
tried in vain to
understand. Suddenly,
a strange hysteria
came over the city.
Men and women rent
their garments and
tore out their hair.
Men threw
themselves upon the
women and raped
them. Fathers and
mothers smashed

gathered up his men
and rode off. No rape
was committed,
no roof torched, not
a drop of blood
spilled. The city
stood in silent
disbelief. For the
longest time, it
wondered why Hajik
had spared it, why
Hajik had turned his
back on his own
legend.

In those days,
Babylon was burying
Nebuchadnezzar.

FATHER:
For hours, Ourgashi
tried in vain to
understand. Suddenly,
a strange hysteria
came over the city.
Men and women rent
their garments and
tore out their hair.
Men threw themselves
upon the women and
raped them. Fathers
and mothers smashed

their children's skulls against the walls of the city. Like cormorants, men and women leapt from the highest towers and disappeared into the waters of the Euphrates. Fire jumped from roof to roof. And so perished Ourgashi the proud, the prosperous, the impenetrable.

MOTHER:
In those days, Babylon was burying Nebuchadnezzar.

In those days, Babylon was burying Nebuchadnezzar.

And even today, on the banks of the Euphrates, people still wonder why Hajik did not take Ourgashi. But I know why. I know! I know! So stop talking! I know that story a thousand times over. But this town isn't Ourgashi...

MOTHER:
In those days, Babylon was burying Nebuchadnezzar.

Shut up, Mama! Shut up! You're not Nebuchadnezzar and

Ikedia isn't Hajik. So
set the fire, Ikedia!

IKEDIA:
Now tell me I'm not
Ikedia.

BABY STAIN:
You are Ikedia. You're
the son of the mask
that sang the dance of
the eldest son of
creation. You are
Ikedia. You're the son
of a man shot down
like a stray dog from a
car window. You are
Ikedia, of the blood-
line deprived of the
right to rest in the
earth, your father's
corpse staring at the
sky, exposed to the
circling vultures
wheeling with
impunity over the
putrefaction of dogs.

*Ikedia moves to the
wall.*

Don't forget it, Ikedia,
so the world won't
forget iteither.

*Ikedia sets the house on
fire.*

Now you're Ikedia.

MOTHER:
Understand first the
firemen first the
firemen right now,
came and shot, in
painful desperate
dance like ashes of
love. Suddenly saw
that never stopped
celebrating, on
Square, my defeat,
really came to shoot
that defeat there.
When shot screamed
in noonday sun,
night suddenly
gathered over city…
Not kill by
accident… Police
better call police
cops too firemen.
Firemen first
firemen. Search
search eyes daughter
caresses father. To
shoot into. Kill eyes,
music made for her
too. His side of her
eyes. "Sweet
little Baby Stain!"
Realize you! Father

You're completely
Ikedia. May the flames
that leap up from this
house bear perpetual
witness to their infamy.

The flames increase.

Now, your bag!

IKEDIA:
What?

BABY STAIN:
Throw your bag in the
fire!

IKEDIA:
No. Somewhere there's
a woman waiting at her
window for a man who
will never return. She
must be released from
her waiting.

BABY STAIN:
Give me that damned
bag, Ikedia. Do you see
that woman? That's my
mother and I slapped
her. She's lost her mind
and I feel nothing but
lightness.

caress her eyes, daughter excite his music: "Sweet little Baby Stain." Police to do police cops too firemen. Firemen first first firemen…

Silence, as if she were aware of the deterioration of her language. Concentrating hard, playing both audience and actress, the mother carries on her private theatre with invisible puppets, the way children play, without seeking anyone's approval, all by herself. Absent. Outside the world, elsewhere.

IKEDIA:
Do what you want with your family. I'll do what I want with mine.

BABY STAIN:
Are you on my side or the world's side? Because I've given everything to you.

IKEDIA:
I'm going where you're going.

BABY STAIN:
Then give me your bag, Ikedia! Stop looking back. *(silence)* Okay, we'll call heads or tails. Papa, do you have a coin? If you win you keep your father's remains; if you lose I throw them into the fire. Heads or tails. Papa, get me a coin.

IKEDIA:
No.

BABY STAIN:
Scaredy-cat!

IKEDIA:
Because I'll win… I always win.

BABY STAIN:
Yeah, I bet! Papa, a coin!

IKEDIA:
No one's going to play dice with my father!

BABY STAIN:
Heads or tails? I'm not going to drag around a coffin for the rest of my life. Papa, a coin! Heads or tails? I take heads. Papa!

MOTHER:
Kn... kn... know... know... Know what happening to you Ikedia sugar? Nice little mousey walking along. See piece cheese. "Incredible! Piece cheese there, nobody watching. Must be dream!" Little mousey rubs two little mousey eyes with two little mousey hands. No, not dream. Good cheesey nice and fresh just for little mousey. Goes like this (imitates mouse steps). Opens mouth (imitates mouse sinking teeth into cheese). Puts teeth in cheese piece not belong anybody. Then all sudden big noise. All dark. Because cheese piece, little sugar sweet

FATHER:
Ikedia, leave your mother the golden prison of hope. Don't take her waiting from her. All your father wants is to be returned to the earth. And the earth is the same everywhere, Ikedia. Dig a grave, anywhere in the garden.

BABY STAIN:
No, not in the garden... not in the garden... Because then we'll have to come back. Even if it's only once in a hundred years. And when I leave, I don't come back.

FATHER:
The earth is the same everywhere, Ikedia. Maybe not in the garden, but return your father to the earth...

Ikedia, is really – ha! ha! ha! – burning hot cat-tongue. Oh yes! And now little mousey caught in cat jaw. But Ikedia, little sugar sweet, pussycat not eat little mousey. Pussycat turn it round and round in black jaws like ear music of prisoner fly in palm of hand. Soon music boring, so pull off wing change tune. But not help. So pull off other wing. Too bad! No more music, all finish, kaput, finitomusic. Not even a little teeny buzz. So open hand and say, "Lazy fly!" and crush it with finger and palm. And that's all, Ikedia, sugar sweet.

BABY STAIN:
This is none of your business, Papa!

BABY STAIN:
Okay, let's go. We'll do it along the way. You won't return him to the earth – I've found something better.

IKEDIA:
This is my decision!

BABY STAIN:
Not any more. From now on, I demand of you what I demand of myself.

IKEDIA:
I'll return his remains to myself... I'll bury him in me...

BABY STAIN:
That's it! Like his mother, the hornbill mask. Now let's fly... let's fly... fly...

FATHER:
For my wife's sake, for mine, for his, return him to the earth. And don't deprive your mother of her waiting...

FATHER:
Aren't you going to say goodbye, Baby Stain?

BABY STAIN:
(*placing her lips on her father's forehead*)
Okay, Ikedia, let's go.

The mother begins to dance the dance of the mask. With an astonishing economy of movement. Almost without moving, around herself, for herself.

BABY STAIN:
We're stepping into the void.

FATHER:
Where will you go?

FATHER:
Ikedia... Will you come back? Even without her, will you come back? (*a beat*) Maybe?

IKEDIA:
Maybe.

FATHER:
Thank you so much, Ikedia, for everything.

MOTHER:
Ikedia my love, my sugar sweet, why that girl after me? Why her? *Her.*

Baby Stain takes Ikedia by the arm; they exit.

FATHER:
Well, the skin has been shed and I've never felt better. Lighter. Lighter. Lighter. Now we'll have to start over again. Start all over. For the next shedding.

The mother dances. Like before. Absent from herself. Movements from within.

Start all over like a prayer to speed his return. He did say "Maybe." Next year. Maybe. He might come back. To tell us the story of the woman waiting at her window for a man who will never return.

He opens his hand. A coin appears. He tosses it into the air. Catches it and slaps it onto the back of his hand.

MOTHER:
Tails! tails! tails! tails! Tails! Tay! tay! tay! tay! tay! tay! tay! T! t! t! t! t! t! t! t... t... t... t... t... t... t... t... t...

FATHER:
He would have won after all. *(a beat)* You could tell me that he walks on water and I'd believe you. A fascinating young man, there's no other word – fascinating. *(turns to the screen where the kiss is still playing)* Look, dear, we're still there.

In the opening in the back wall surrounded by flames, the mask appears. It dances so airily, so slowly that the back wall seems to be a silent screen.

BLACK OUT

About the playwright:

Koffi Kwahulé was born in 1956 in Abengourou (Ivory Coast). He studied at the Institut National des Arts in Abidjan, at l'École de la rue Blanche (Paris), and at the Sorbonne Nouvelle (Paris) where he earned his doctorate in Theatre Studies. Jazz has always greatly influenced and inspired both the form and content of his writing. He is the author of more than twenty plays including *Cette vieille magie noire* (recipient of the Grand prix Tchicaya U Tam'si, RFI/ACCT, 1992); *La dame du café d'en face* (recipient of Prix SACD-RFI, 1994); *Bintou*; *Fama*; *Les créanciers*; *Village fou ou Les déconnards* (recipient of the Priz UNESCO du MASA 1999); *Il nous faut l'Amérique*; *Jaz*; *Big shoot*; *P'tite Souillure* (winner of the prestigious Journées d'Auteurs de Lyons 2002); *Histoires de soldats* and *Scat. Blue-S-cat* and *Misterioso-119* are his most recent works. His plays have been published by the Éditions Théâtrales, Lansman, Actes Sud-Papiers, and Acoria, produced in Europe, Africa and North America and have been translated into several languages.

About the translator:

Born in Chicago, living in Montreal, **David Homel** is one of Canada's best-known literary translators and the winner of two Governor-General's Awards in that category. The writers he has translated include Dany Laferrière, Daniel Pennac and Martine Desjardins. He is also a novelist and the author of six award-winning works of fiction that have been published in several countries. David Homel also works as a documentary film-maker and a journalist in both of Canada's official languages.

THE LAST MORNING

(Le Complexe de Thénardier)

By José Pliya

Translated by
Maureen LaBonté

Production Information:

Le Complexe de Thénardier was first read at the Festival d'Avignon during the summer of 2001. The reading was staged by Jean-Michel Ribes and featured Catherine Hiegel and Sylvie Testud. It went on to be premiered at the Théâtre du Rond-Point (Paris) in November of 2002, again directed by Jean-Michel Ribes with Marilu Marini and Laure Calamy.

The Last Morning was read in workshop at both the 2002 and the 2003 Banff playRites Colonies by, Gay Hauser, Jenny Young, Carmen Grant and Valerie Pearson. Linda Gaboriau acted as translation dramaturge on both occasions.

The Last Morning was also read as part of the National Arts Centre's (Ottawa) *International Reading Series* in November 2003. Keith Turnbull directed with Carol Anderson and Ngozi Paul reading.

The Thénardier complex does exist.
In the last century, there was evidence of it in occupied Europe, in
Rwanda, in the former Yugoslavia…
And, back home, in the house where I grew up.

José Pliya

For Jeanne, Léila, Blanche, Ida, Amssatou, Julie and all the other
little hands here and elsewhere.

EPILOGUE

VIDO:

Madam. You fell asleep. Don't stay there like that. Lying on the floor. In the middle of the living room. You'd be more comfortable in your bed. You're exhausted. Staying up all night, keeping watch, has tired you. You're asleep. You're asleep. Here's your throw. Keep covered. Rest. Madam. Rest. There. I'm ready. I made myself pretty. A little lipstick. I'm taking my old coat. It must be cold out. I'm leaving. I'm happy. Despite everything. There were good times. I have no regrets. Thank you. I'm going to look for my father. I'm going to look for my mother. There may be some hope of finding them. We'll come back to see you. I promise. I also wanted to say: maybe I lied. I don't know anymore. I don't know anymore whether I saw him, the blue soldier, or whether I dreamt it. My handsome soldier with the blue hair and the accent. The heavy Dakota accent. I can still hear him telling me that he'd be here, now, to take me away with him. It's past the time. He isn't here. I must have dreamt it. I'm sorry. There. I'm going. You're asleep. I won't have your blessing. That's alright. I'll be back.

THE MOTHER:

Good morning, Vido. The chair legs, today. In the living room, use the soft cloth. The living room chairs are fragile. And don't forget the ones in the kitchen. You've forgotten them twice now. You do the tops but not the legs. There are black stains. You can see them. Pay attention. Don't waste cleaner. It's impossible to find these days. I'll say it again, if I have to: all you need is a tiny amount, the tiniest drop, a tear drop. That's all it takes for four legs. You rub, the stains disappear. You can't find that cleaner anymore. No cleaner in the living room. I've told you a hundred times. It's toxic. The chairs are walnut. It damages them. You don't listen. A soft cloth and hydrogen peroxide on the living room chairs.

VIDO:

Good morning, Auntie. I wish you a good, good morning. Accept my greeting with warmth and friendship the way you would a fond farewell. Good morning.

THE MOTHER:

I said good morning. Now, pay attention. There are mildew stains in the bathroom. Open your eyes. That's all that's asked of you. I'm tired of repeating. It's like all the rest: the dishes, the washing, the cooking. Nothing's finished. Everything's the same, sloppy, half-done. The more I repeat, the less you do. Igor is complaining that his stomach hurts. Indigestion, I suppose. It must be. These days anything that goes into the mouth must be disinfected. Fruit, vegetables, everything. There's no more baking soda. Of course, you didn't tell me. That's too much to ask. The result: Igor's not well. You drive me crazy, Vido. Crazy. What do I have to say to get through to you.

VIDO:

May every blessing imaginable rain down on you and your family: health, happiness, prosperity. I also want to thank you. For feeding me, for clothing me and for saving my life. I've come to say thank you.

THE MOTHER:

I'm not asking for the moon. Just let me know ahead of time. About the potatoes, the oil, the salt, the onions. Just let me know and if at all possible don't make us sick. Everything's always so complicated with you. So dramatic. I'll bring back some baking soda. Now. You take a pan. Pour in some water and mix. You don't need a lot of water. You soak the food. All the food. One full hour. No more no less. You throw out the water and rinse everything. The rats are back because of your negligence. The rats. My god, the rats. What did we do to deserve them. You can hear them in the cupboards, under the armchairs, behind the doors. You can hear them and they don't die. Carelessness. That's what it is.

VIDO:

Kiss each of your children for me. They've given me so much joy. Tell them I love them. Kiss Snejana for me. Pretty Snejana.

MOTHER:

The children are about to wake up. Bring the chicory, the bread, a knife, the sugar, the brown sugar and the butter. I have to ask, every morning. And water for Igor's pills. He won't have slept well. He has to keep taking his medicine. I brought him back some cigarettes, beer, magazines. He has to rest. Make sure that he doesn't go out. He'll try to. Stop him. Be firm. He mustn't go out. He doesn't know what it's like out there. If they get their hands on him, they'll kill him. Like that. No questions asked. He has no idea. He wants to fight. He wants to fight. Poor child.

VIDO:

I'm going to miss Snejana. I miss her already. My heart is heavy. Let me tell you again how grateful I am to you. How infinitely grateful.

THE MOTHER:

Today for lunch, you'll shell the peas and cook the meat. Mind the fat. Wash your hands properly. I asked for the bread. You're too slow. You're too soft. And a glass of water. I'm going to bed now. Get to work in the house. In the bathroom, don't forget the Javex for the bath, the sink, the toilet. In the living room, the dust. In the laundry, there's handwashing to do: the whites. Remember to wring well. You have specific jobs to do in this house. Do them properly. Be responsible.

VIDO:

I'm going to cry. I know it. I know what I'm like. I swore I wouldn't, or if I did, I'd hide behind my hands so it wouldn't show. It's no use. I'm going to cry anyway.

THE MOTHER:

You're very trying, Vido. You talk too much. Your coffee's no good. I've just gotten in. I haven't slept all night. I'm tired. There were gunshots. There are more and more now. Patrols too. They prowl, they check, they stop people. More and more. Night and day. No one is safe. No one. You talk too much, Vido. You get on my nerves.

VIDO:

Auntie, what I have to say to you I say in all humility. The humility of my station. The humility of my education. What I'm trying to say isn't easy. I'll say it simply, with my eyes lowered as a sign of respect. Look at me: I'm not looking at you. Listen to me: I hardly dare whisper I'm so afraid to offend you. I don't want to hurt you. I owe you my life. I never raise my voice and I

back out of the room. I don't have a way with words. That's true.
I find it very hard. Especially saying goodbye. I didn't want to
face you like this. I'd have preferred not to. Not because I'm
afraid of you but because I'm afraid of speaking, afraid of myself
and my tears. If I knew how to write, I would have left long
before dawn and you would've "read me." That would've been so
much easier. As if I'd left the morning after you first took me in.
But I don't know how to write. So here I am with my words and
my gratitude and I've come to ask your permission to leave.

THE MOTHER:

That's fine, Vido, fine. You can go now. Clear the table later. You
have more important things to do in the kitchen. Go. I'm tired.

VIDO:

I always knew that it wouldn't be simple. It's my own fault. It's
my own fault if people don't understand me. I'm so awkward
with words. If it weren't so bold, so presumptuous of me, I'd say:
look at your house. Things can speak more eloquently than
words. Look at your house. How clean it is, washed, swept,
polished, dusted, bleached, ironed, tidied, prepared. Like it's
never been before. Look. A new house, for a new beginning. To
mark the end of my time here. These are my words. Look. There.
Look at my parting words. My goodbye. But I knew you'd have
trouble understanding. Forgive me, Auntie. I don't mean to be
disrespectful. Forgive me.

THE MOTHER:

I forgive you, Vido. You've been through so much. Seen so much.
I forgive all your chatter. But don't try to take advantage of me.
Get to work now. It'll be light soon.

VIDO:

You're going to make me explain. I don't want to. But I'll have to.
Explain myself, argue, discuss and I don't want to offend you by

doing that. Order me to leave. I respect your authority, use it. Let's pretend none of this has happened. It's morning. You come home. The table is set. The children are asleep. You call for me. I don't answer. I'm gone. No questions, no interrogation. I've left and that's that. Let's do it that way. But, it's too late I'm afraid. I've said too much, or not enough or I've said it really badly. And I'm ashamed when I see myself insisting, telling you to do this or asking you to order me to do that. I don't want to. I don't want to.

THE MOTHER:

That's enough. Get to work. You're wasting my time. You're incoherent. Enough.

VIDO:

You're forcing me to explain. I'd have done anything to avoid it. I guess it was inevitable. I'll try to erase myself. Become an absence. Relieve you of a burden. There'll only be my voice. As soft as a whisper. Without a hint of impertinence. I pray that you'll forgive my impertinence.

THE MOTHER:

Vido, my patience is running out.

VIDO:

Auntie, I'm going away. I'm leaving you. For good. Give me your blessing.

THE MOTHER:

That's enough.

VIDO:

I saw a man. A man with blue hair. He told me it was all over. He's coming to take me away with him. He has an accent. He's from Dakota. He has a strong Dakota accent. He was very clear. The war is over. We're free. We're free.

THE MOTHER:

That's enough. You're not making any sense. The war isn't over. There is no man. You never see anyone. You don't know anyone. You never go out. You had a bad dream. That's all. Remember when you first arrived here: you had nightmares. You used to dream about the prophet Ezekiel coming to save you and your family. You're like that. You've a touch of the mystic, of the visionary. You've been through so much. There is no man. You had a bad dream.

VIDO:

It wasn't a dream. He came to me. He sat right there, in your place. You were out. The door was closed. The children asleep. I don't know how he got in. He was right there. I made coffee. He likes my coffee. He talked about peace, brotherhood, love. He says we're going to have to learn how to live again. That we'll have to forgive. Dispense justice, not forget, but still forgive. Lots of words. I have trouble with words. I looked at him. He was handsome. He smelled like the plains of Dakota. I'm free.

THE MOTHER:

You're not free. You're talking nonsense. There is no liberation. I would know. We've been waiting for them to free us for ages. They've forgotten about us. The war isn't over. Just the opposite. There are more massacres and executions than ever. You'll only hurt yourself by believing in this insanity. It's gone to your head. It's muddled your thinking.

VIDO:

I'm honoured by your concern. I'm very moved. I've nothing to fear, not anymore, believe me. I know I'm protected and I'm leaving here at peace.

THE MOTHER:

You're not leaving. I forbid it. I didn't save you from genocide to lose you now for no good reason, all because of a bad dream. I'll tell you what this is about. It's Snejana. She's been talking to you. I should have kept quiet, not said a word to her. Not fed her dreams of resistance. My daughter talked to you about the white torpedoes, didn't she? There've been lots of false rumours started by the Resistance to destabilize the government. Makes them jumpy. The latest are about UN intervention, troops landing, liberation. False rumours to spread panic. Makes them feel cornered. No good ever comes of it. In the end, everyone suffers: rationing, patrols, arrests, and still more terror. You fight the best you can. And, Vido, the only way for you to fight is to stay hidden. The war isn't over.

VIDO:
The war is over. The man with the blue hair told me so and I believe him. And even if it's not true, I still want to believe it. It's something beautiful to hope for in the cloistered life I live here. I have to get out. See the sun face to face. See the flowers. I have to leave here.

THE MOTHER:
I forbid it. If you go out there, you're dead. If you walk around, you're dead. Dead before you say one word to the first person you meet. Get this through your head: you don't exist out there. They have chosen to deny any trace of your humanity. You know: like a child who erases a beautiful drawing because he thinks it's not finished or it's flawed, or missing something. So, he erases it with care, systematically, methodically because he wants the page to be pure and white again. But there are still smudges all over it, smudges the child can't seem to get out and so he gets angry. He erases and erases and erases. He scrapes his eraser over the page until he rips it. Rips it to pieces.

VIDO:

And I'm that smudge. A smudge on a page of History. Something a child throws in the garbage like an orange peel and that you picked up, hid, sheltered and fed. God bless you for that. No, I haven't forgotten who I am or who I was, since I'm not allowed to exist anymore. But I've buried myself in your hospitality for too long. I can't stand it anymore. I'm suffocating. I need to breathe so that I know I'm still alive. And if, as you say – and I don't want to doubt your word – the fighting hasn't stopped, then let me fight too.

THE MOTHER:

There we are. I knew it was all that talk with the children. They've influenced you. Fight. Poor fools. You have no idea. That's not war out there. It's slaughter. Slaughter with only one purpose: total extermination. The extermination of your people. There's no code of good behaviour, no laws, no rules. Nothing but death for you, your people and anyone close to you. We don't need you to become some kind of martyr. What's the good of that. And your parents, if they've survived, will need you when all this is over.

VIDO:

My father. A tall man with the hands of a logger. Of a woodsman. Twinkling eyes, always smiling. A man of few words. An austere man but with the softest eyes. He lived for his wife, his daughter, his shop. The shop on the corner. It was his whole life, that shop. Greeting the customers, taking inventory, filling orders and, most important, never be too greedy. Make just enough to get by. Money breeds misery he used to say. It drove my mother crazy. But she was right. He had a gold mine on his hands. His big logger's hands. When they took him away, he didn't say a word. He touched me on the shoulder. A furtive touch. A caress. That hand protects me and follows me. That hand watches over me. My mother. She was never made to be happy. She loved too much. She was too female, too maternal, too religious, too full of fear. She predicted it all. She saw it coming. I remember. It was a market day. She looked at the butchered animals and saw killing fields covered with bones, skulls crawling with flies. The market turned into horror and atrocities right before her eyes. That much insight in one woman. It was too much. How do you live with that.

THE MOTHER:

Your parents are alive. Just yesterday, I read you a letter from them. They're alive. It's a miracle and a sign. You have to survive and be reunited. Later. Much later, when everything is over. Not now. Stop all this nonsense. It's time we put an end to this discussion. It's absurd. A waste of time. I've let myself be taken in by all your chatter. It's contagious. Look at us going on like two old biddies bickering about the end of the world. You're irritating, Vido. Incredibly irritating.

VIDO:

My heart is on its knees. I can't tell you how confused I am. In the letter you read me yesterday from my father, I heard his advice to me: "Be a good girl, Vido. Don't forget how we brought you up. Always be polite, quiet, obedient. Keep your eyes lowered, don't argue, don't talk back. Do what you're told. Don't ever demand. You're very lucky. Auntie saved your life." I'm so torn. Please give me your permission to go.

THE MOTHER:

You don't have my permission. Don't expect me to give it to you. I will not be an accomplice to your suicide. I'm thinking of your parents. One day, no doubt, they'll be free. They'll come here. They'll come here to claim you. And no matter how I try to explain. No matter what I say they won't believe me. Even if I tell them it came over you, like that, one sad winter morning. Out of the blue. They won't believe me. They won't believe me and that would be understandable: survivors never accept the death of their loved ones. No, you do not have my permission.

VIDO:

I beg you. I could have left without making a sound like my handsome soldier asked me to. I could have slipped away, run off like a criminal. In the dead of night. I stayed. Like a good little girl. I waited. I need your blessing. When my father and I used to leave on trips, my mother would sit us down in the back room of the shop and there, surrounded by cartons and shelves with dust all around us, she would lay her hands on us. She would bless us. Only then, could we leave. I need your blessing.

THE MOTHER:

You're not a child anymore. You're a woman. But still, I could be your mother. So, let's suppose you're my daughter, my eldest daughter. Igor is your younger brother. Jana, the baby. Let's suppose. You're under my authority. And since the day it started, I've taken care to shelter you from the barbarity. All of that out there is not for you. Not for my three children. You're the eldest, grown up, independent and your mind's made up. You decide to go fight. Against my advice. Faced with the inevitable, I'm powerless, a mother already in mourning for her child. In a last, desperate effort, before you do something irreparable, I find the words: "We're a family, Vido. You have rights, but you also have duties. Your duty as the eldest is to set a good example. Your brother and sister will follow you, if you leave. Follow your example. For Igor, for Snejana, don't leave."

VIDO:

Forgive me. All the charity you've shown me doesn't make you my mother. All the affection I feel for you doesn't make me your daughter. People don't chose their children. They accept them with open arms, a gift for life and beyond. You saved my life, you didn't give it to me. I had a place in your house, the place I deserved. And now, in your goodness, you've elevated me to the rank of eldest child. Suddenly I'm heir to your love. It's overwhelming. I agree to be your daughter. Your prodigal daughter. And as such, I claim my share of your children's inheritance: your blessing.

THE MOTHER:
I can't go along with this madness.

VIDO:
My leaving affects no one but me.

THE MOTHER:
You'll incriminate us all.

VIDO :
You're trying to make me responsible for something that has nothing to do with me.

THE MOTHER:
It's the truth.

VIDO:
I can't accept that. I can't believe that you'll suffer because of me.

THE MOTHER:
You'll be stopped, arrested, tortured.

VIDO:
...

THE MOTHER:
Before killing you, they'll question you. Believe me, you'll talk.

VIDO:
...

THE MOTHER:
You'll talk about me, how I took you in.

VIDO:
…

THE MOTHER:
You'll talk about Igor, my big baby.

VIDO:
…

THE MOTHER:
You'll betray Jana, your little Snejana.

VIDO:
…

THE MOTHER:
You'll put us all in danger.

VIDO:
I won't be made responsible for this.

THE MOTHER:
You don't have a monopoly on suffering.

VIDO:
This is not what I wanted. I was leaving with my mind at peace because I knew the three of you were safe. I said to myself, we're free now, they have nothing to fear anymore. And even if we aren't free, they have nothing to fear. This house is protected.

THE MOTHER:
You were wrong. You invited that stranger into our house, without knowing him. What were you thinking. Where was your

common sense. I hold that against you, Vido. I hold it against you.

VIDO:

If I told you that you have nothing to fear from me, you wouldn't believe me. If I told you that even under torture I wouldn't give you away, you wouldn't believe me. That's normal, you're a mother. All the same, it's true. I have nothing to confess. I don't know anything about what you do out there at night or during the day for that matter. I've shared your children's laughter and their silences. I have nothing to say. There is nothing to say. You can't confess to nothing.

MOTHER:

You'll confess. They have ways. You'll confess to anything and it will be like a deliverance. You'll discover within yourself a talent you never knew you had. Drunk with pain, your imagination will know no bounds. Jana will be a terrorist, Igor a resistance fighter and I'll be Mata Hari. Hallucinating, you'll describe in minute detail how our organization operates: the building of bombs in the basement by the light of a hurricane lamp, attacks of surgical precision on strategic targets: bridges, barracks, police headquarters. How many senior officers we've eliminated. You'll catch yourself enjoying it. With a kind of morbid pleasure you'll add details until we become the heroes of a fictional resistance movement. You will be our executioner.

VIDO:

...

THE MOTHER:

I know you, Vido. You're a good girl. Lazy by nature, a bit flighty, but hardworking. Over all, I have nothing to complain about.

VIDO:

> ...

THE MOTHER:

> You're clean. The house is not too badly kept. Except for the rats
> this last while. The rats are a nuisance.

VIDO:

> ...

THE MOTHER:

> You haven't seen to the rats. You have to put rat poison
> everywhere: the gas stove, the pantry, the garbage bins.

VIDO:

> ...

THE MOTHER:

> You're honest. That's important. We can trust you. Except for
> that stranger in my living room. That's totally unacceptable.

VIDO:

> ...

THE MOTHER:

> I don't believe that story. I don't believe a word of it. You're
> a dreamer. You let yourself get carried away sometimes. It's
> a tendancy of yours. You don't mean anything by it.
> Harmless really.

VIDO:

> ...

THE MOTHER:

> You're not pretty and you let that bother you. You shouldn't.

Beauty isn't everything. You're not unattractive. Children
like you.

VIDO

...

THE MOTHER:

I know you.

VIDO:

I'm touched by your description of me. If that's how you see me,
that must be the way I am. Thank you for the compliments.
They're the first I've ever had. I accept them.

THE MOTHER:

You have faults. We all do. You're secretive. Maybe even a bit
sneaky. You're not straightforward enough.

VIDO:

...

THE MOTHER:

Say what you have to say more clearly. All this fancy talk of
yours has been a waste of time. You lack simplicity.

VIDO:

...

THE MOTHER:

You're too obsequious. Get to the point. Stop making such a
fuss. It's not necessary. I understood perfectly well what you
were after.

VIDO:

...

THE MOTHER:

All you had to do was make me a proposition. I would've listened to it, thought about it. We would have discussed it.

VIDO:

…

THE MOTHER:

I'm open. I'm a woman. I can understand your frustrations. I can arrange things for you. But you have to speak up.

VIDO:

…

THE MOTHER:

You're willing to stay here and work for me. But you want some sort of compensation. Something more tangible perhaps. There's nothing mysterious about that. You should've just said so.

VIDO:

…

THE MOTHER:

I'm warning you though: I have no money. I can't pay you. But, we can negotiate.

VIDO:

I came here, to your house, by accident. During all those years it took me to recover, I couldn't stand around doing nothing. I wanted to clean the house and help in the kitchen. It wasn't my calling, what I was meant to do in life. It happened by accident. But by working for you I rebuilt myself. A little. I created order in my pain. And in the household tasks that I performed day after day, over and over again, I found a reason to hope.

THE MOTHER:
You see. You are complicated. Without even knowing what I have to offer, you're raising the stakes. Listen to me.

VIDO:
I'm listening, Auntie.

THE MOTHER:
Here's my offer - Igor.

VIDO:
I'm afraid I don't understand.

THE MOTHER:
I'm offering you my son, Igor. You're in love. He marries you and you stay. You stay here in this house, run the household, and make us babies.

VIDO:
…

THE MOTHER:
Don't pretend to be naive. We both know how old you are. Your chances of meeting someone now are pretty slim. This is a real opportunity for you.

VIDO:
…

THE MOTHER:
Igor's a good-looking man. Weak and cowardly like all men, but he'll be able to make you babies. And you won't have to sneak around to make love anymore.

VIDO:
…

THE MOTHER:

I'll take care of the children's education. Igor's not capable and you'll have your work to do. You needn't concern yourself about any of that. I'll look after it.

VIDO:

…

THE MOTHER:

Don't say anything. My offer probably comes as a total surprise. But it's not, if you stop and think about it. It's the natural result of living in such close quarters. Think about it. We'll talk again tomorrow.

VIDO:

You've misunderstood me. There's no love between your son and me. I could be his mother. He's been my lover. It happened one evening at the beginning of the war. You weren't home and he was crying. He told me about the rats when he was little. The rats that would come and nibble at his finger tips. And about his screaming and how no one could calm him or comfort him. Not you. Not his father. He cried and I consoled him and he made love to me. He was gentle and warm and patient. And ever since then, I can't resist him. He has a way about him. When I'm with him I forget everything. He turns me inside out. I like that. Every time. But it's not love. It's desire.

THE MOTHER:

I used the word love because I didn't want to hurt your feelings. You don't love my son. He doesn't love you. That's just as well. We'll be able to reach an understanding. Desire is much easier to bargain with.

VIDO:

You offend me, Auntie. Our desire is not for sale. What happened between Igor and me was passion. Sexual passion. We're not for sale.

THE MOTHER:

> Don't kid yourself. Everything is for sale. You thought my son's cries of pleasure were a sign of deep sexual satisfaction. Well, you were wrong. This passion you feel for him is by no means mutual. Igor is your lover because I wanted him to be. His desire, an order. Purely mechanical. Everything is for sale. Everything can be bought. Everything. There. Now you know.

VIDO:

> ...

THE MOTHER:

> You're devastated. You shouldn't be. You're naive, Vido. Don't ask men to give what they're not capable of giving. A man comes and goes, leaves, returns, but never stays. You must learn to know them. Then, you won't be disappointed. A man can be useful for a night, if you need someone to hold you I suppose. But that's about it. And that's not bad.

VIDO:

> ...

THE MOTHER:

> I know you can be greedy. You're the child of shopkeepers after all. But don't hesitate too long. You're smart. What I'm offering you is a position in life. Roots that will prevent you from wandering aimlessly. After the war. Think about it.

VIDO:

> ...

THE MOTHER:

> You may go now.

VIDO:

> ...

THE MOTHER:
I said you may go now.

VIDO:
...

THE MOTHER:
Please.

VIDO:
...

THE MOTHER:
Vido, I'm talking to you.

VIDO:
...

THE MOTHER:
All right. Obviously, we have a problem here.

VIDO:
...

THE MOTHER:
You have a problem.

VIDO:
...

THE MOTHER:
We'll talk about it. But, you must obey me.

VIDO:
...

THE MOTHER:
You're defying me, Vido. I don't like that.

VIDO:
...

THE MOTHER:
I don't like that look.

VIDO:
...

THE MOTHER:
Lower your eyes.

VIDO:
...

THE MOTHER:
Lower your eyes when you look at me.

VIDO:
...

THE MOTHER:
Please.

VIDO:
...

THE MOTHER:
Thank you.

VIDO:
...

THE MOTHER:
Don't provoke me.

VIDO:
…

THE MOTHER:
Ever again.

VIDO:
…

THE MOTHER:
Ever again.

VIDO:
…

THE MOTHER:
Thank you.

VIDO:
…

THE MOTHER:
You wanted to talk to me.

VIDO:
…

THE MOTHER:
I'm listening.

VIDO:

We don't know each other. It takes a war to make us realize it. We've lived in the same house without knowing each other. Side by side. Two solitudes lost in the noise of the cannons. A very long monologue with almost no interruptions. We don't know each other. I came to you today showing deference and you saw cunning. I spoke to you with gratitude, you heard greed. I hoped for your blessing, you offered me some kind of deal. We don't understand each other.

THE MOTHER:

That's going too far, Vido. All I'm suggesting is an exchange of services. Nothing more. Simple and straightforward. The kind of transaction that goes on between two women all the time. Hundreds. Every day down in the market. At the peep of dawn. My offer's no different. If it doesn't suit you, say so. I've lots more in my basket: dainty ones, tasty ones, rich and luscious ones that will make you forget you ever thought of leaving us.

VIDO:

...

THE MOTHER:

I've got something for every taste: lascivious, twisted, indirect but deadly. I'm not forcing you. I'm suggesting. Here's one: I could've demanded that you restore the house to what it was when you got here. Asked that before you leave you return it to its original filth. The same grime that was on the curtains before you bleached them clean. The original dirt. I'd be within my rights. I could've demanded it and you would have had no choice.

VIDO:

...

THE MOTHER:

Or, how about this one: before leaving get rid of the rats for me. We didn't have any before you got here. Since then, they've multiplied. No one sees them but they're there. I suspect you of hiding them. The poison disappears but they don't. You're behind it somehow. Rats in such a clean house. Impossible. As long as there's a single rat left, you don't leave. I could've suggested that.

VIDO:

...

THE MOTHER:

And, finally, a perverse one: I could have demanded that you pack up and remove the pain, the suffering and the long funeral procession of fear that you dragged into this house and that has haunted it for so many years. I could have.

VIDO:

...

THE MOTHER:

I treated you like an equal by offering you the very best of me. I offered you my son. You're provoking me.

VIDO:

You shouldn't have, madam. I knew where I stood. I had my own hierarchy. You were at the top. Way up there. Now with this deal of yours, my world is crumbling. I don't know where I stand anymore because of you.

THE MOTHER:

I don't like your tone, my girl. I don't like your choice of words. I spoke to you with the best of intentions, without animosity. Don't provoke me.

VIDO:

I wouldn't know how. That's not how I was brought up. I'm upset, Madam. Upset by the feelings my leaving has aroused. Upset by your concern to save me from a war that I believe is over. Upset by your desire to protect me against my will. Upset by your need to keep me here with you. All this upsets me a lot.

THE MOTHER:

That's going too far. It's because you got it into your head to leave. That's what caused all this. Pull yourself together. I made you an offer. It doesn't suit you. Fine. I take it back. Nothing happened. Don't exaggerate. Don't turn it into something it's not. Nothing's happened.

VIDO:

Oh yes, Madam, something is happening. The thought of my leaving bothers you. I can see that. You've used kindness and advice, guilt and bargaining. One after the other. And now you're threatening me. Please, explain.

THE MOTHER:

You're asking to leave, I won't let you. You want my approval, you don't have it. You do not have my permission.

VIDO:

Madam, please explain.

THE MOTHER:

There's nothing to explain. That's the way it is. I'm confiscating your papers: id cards, permits, passport. I'm detaining you.

VIDO:

Madam, please explain.

THE MOTHER:

I'm denying you your right to understand. Last official address: unknown. Height: unknown. Colour of eyes: unknown. Your exit visa is no longer valid.

VIDO:

Madam, please explain.

THE MOTHER:

I'm confiscating your identity. You no longer have a name: a family name or a first name. You don't even have a nationality. There is no place in this land that holds a memory of you. No date, no place, no birth.

VIDO:

Madam, please explain.

THE MOTHER:

From this day on, you're under house arrest. Don't touch the keys. Keep away from the doors. Don't open the windows not even to shake out the tablecloth. You're confined to this house.

VIDO:

…

THE MOTHER:

From now on, you'll get up even earlier. Before dawn. You'll go to bed even later. After nightfall. Between the two, you'll work, cook, clean. Eat after we do. Drink after we do. And you will not laugh.

VIDO:

…

THE MOTHER:

I don't want any more broken glasses. I don't want any more broken plates. And I want you to do an inventory of the china every week. You'll use your own toilet, the one by the back door. There will be no more sex. You will abstain. Totally. Become a nun.

VIDO:

...

THE MOTHER:

Lock up your dreams of leaving. You will not be leaving. Forget the plains of Dakota and the thousand hills. Forget fresh air and freedom. There will always be a war to keep you here. You will not be leaving.

VIDO:

...

THE MOTHER:

Stop crying. I can't stand your tears. Can't you at least howl and wail like those women hired to cry at funerals. I loathe your silent tears. They're hypocritical.

VIDO:

...

THE MOTHER:

I warn you. One day, you'll think of running away. One day, you'll think of escaping. It's tempting. It will happen. If you do, I warn you: you'll regret it. That's a promise.

VIDO:

...

THE MOTHER:

I will denounce you. It's called informing. Informing is a mean,
self-serving, contemptible act, done in secret, generally by night,
like hyenas at the edge of the forest. I will do it calmly, with no
second thoughts, no scruples, maybe even with a hint of pleasure.
The intoxication of betrayal. At the break of day, at that hour
when the streetlights are still breathing the evening dew, I'll
skulk along the still-damp walls. The streets will be deserted
because of the curfew and I'll take pleasure in this small
transgression, in the hope, the morbid hope, that I'll be arrested
or maybe even shot. On the spot, no questions asked. But that
won't happen. I'll meet the she-dogs of dawn, packs of them on
their way home after a night of debauchery, of bacchanalian
orgies, couplings in mud-filled ditches. Their stomachs heavy,
their lips red with blood. They'll recognize me as one of theirs.
We'll recognize one another. Carrion. Friends. I'll get through
every blockade and every check point. I won't have to explain a
thing. The guards will know: they can smell an informer. It's a
very popular smell these days. A heady perfume, with just a hint
of pestilence. Easy to get used to. I'll clear every checkpoint
without a second thought. There'll be no telltale sign, no cock's
crow, no siren, no call to moral order. I won't tremble. My voice
will be calm, serene, at ease with its lies. I'll denounce you.
Casually. Without brutality. Aware that I'm part of an ancient
tradition. A human tradition. I'll spell your name, letter by letter,
syllable by syllable, like an actress doing a diction exercise.
V.I.D.O.M.I.N.G.O.N., Vi-do-min-gon, a lowly sewer she-rat who,
without my knowledge, Your Honour, insinuated herself into my
house. When I found her, she reeked of misery, a sad sorry sight.
My heart went out to her and so I took her in, Your Honour. I
couldn't stand the thought that she was being hunted down. In
no time, she insinuated herself everywhere: the kitchen, the attic,
the living room, the dining room. She took over. Her and her
kind. You know what these creatures are like, Your Honour,
they're lustful and insatiable. She chose a male for herself, a weak

and cowardly individual, but he impregnated her. Now they're everywhere. A colony of rats, your Honour. They multiply despite the traps and the poison. What I have here, Your Honour, is an excellent rat poison. Fast. Effective. It doesn't kill them. They're invisible. No matter how hard I fight back, my house is no longer my own. My house is an occupied zone. I don't know what to do anymore. I'm afraid, Your Honour. I'm afraid. And that's why I'm handing her over to you. Her name is Vido. Remember that name: Vido. You'll find her. If you capture her, the other rats will give themselves up. I know I can count on you. You'll catch them and you'll know how to eliminate them. Your methods are better than traps or poison. I've been told about your methods: on their knees, hands behind the neck, a bullet through the head. No rat can survive that. I've also heard about the gas, the gas pumped down the sewers. A colony of rats can't survive that. I know I can count on you. I'm done now, Your Honour. I'm done. And then I'd leave. I'd go back home, as if nothing had happened. An ordinary morning like any other. A pale sun will be warming the wet cobblestones. The same guards who were there earlier will be waiting for the day shift to replace them. They'll smile and offer me coffee. I'll hurry along. The streets will start to get busier. Over there, a grocer and his turnips. And right here, a line-up in front of the baker's. Far off, we can hear the dim echo of a firing squad, quickly covered by the songs of the sparrows. I'll enter my house. The door will creak. I'll put on my slippers. Hang up my coat to dry. I'll drink a glass of water or maybe a glass of milk. Through the window, a pale, monotonous ray of sunshine will fall across the living room. I'll go into my bedroom, crawl between the sheets, under my blanket, and before I fall asleep, I'll hear soft snores coming from the children's room. I'll fall asleep. It will be an ordinary morning. An ordinary morning in a world at war.

VIDO:

. . .

THE MOTHER:

You may go now.

VIDO:

You saved my life. You're one of the Just, madam, a saint. I nearly
believed you. For a brief moment there, I was suddenly riddled
with doubt. It gripped me like a toothache. And I doubted you. I
doubted your hands. So beautiful, so slim. Hands that have done
so much good and never boasted. I doubted your eyes which can
be hard and severe and yet I've seen them cry many, many times
like a lonely, shamefaced little girl who's been caught out. I
doubted your voice, the voice that said "Come in" when I was
fleeing death on a night of raids. I doubted. A strange thing
doubt, based on nothing or very little. I nearly believed you.

THE MOTHER:

Poor fool. You'd be wise to trust your doubt. Might be more
reliable than appearances. You don't know me. My hands have
caressed so many uniforms, my eyes have looked away from so
many crimes, my lips have kissed so many boots. It's beyond
imagining. So hush. You don't know me.

VIDO:

You saved my life. I can doubt anything but not that. When I
entered your house I entered a safe haven. A parenthesis of life at
the heart of a storm. We're sheltered here. Sheltered from need.
Nothing is lacking. There's always plenty. Bread, lard, drinking
water and light. And your children. Your children's laughter. Like
me, happiness has found a refuge in your house.

THE MOTHER:

You'll never know the concessions that have to be made to create
an illusion of happiness. The concessions, the sacrifices, the
cowardice and the baseness required to preserve that illusion.
When it all started, I had a choice. Like everyone else. Live or

die. Of hunger. I'm a mother. I have two mouths to feed. I'm
alone. I didn't hesitate: like a coyote, I went out hunting
and I took what I was given where I could find it. In the camp
of horror.

VIDO:

We owe you our lives. Not one or two, but three lives saved.
Snejana has the soul of a rebel, a born fighter. She would have
gone off to fight. She would have joined the resistance. She
would have been killed. Igor too. He grumbles, he storms, he
bullies. He likes to play the man of the house but he's weak
and cowardly. Not cut out for war. Tomorrow, in a few days,
in a while, all this will be over. They'll be free, they'll be alive
and they'll understand and appreciate everything you've done
for them.

THE MOTHER:

I've run with the coyotes. Both my children know that. If they're
asked, they'll testify. My daughter has a noble heart, a sense of
honour. She blames me for everything. I see it in her eyes. She
hates me. She'll say nothing: neither for nor against me. She won't
defend me. And my son. My son. He'll say what he's told to say.
He'll do what he's told to do. He'll denounce me along with my
judges and cast the first stone on my shaved head. My son. A
man, a real man. I'm a collaborator. And if I had to do it again,
I would.

VIDO:

I owe you my life. I know what you did that winter night. It was
spontaneous, unselfish, pure. A human response. Behind me,
there's more than me. There's my father, my mother, my kin.
You've saved more than just me. You've saved a people. We'll be
your witnesses.

THE MOTHER:

I didn't save you. I exploited you. You were a gold mine landing at my feet. A treasure from my childhood. War is no different than life, there are no heroes and no monsters. There are only men and women struggling with themselves and their pasts. I'm exploiting you, Vido. I'm using you to be everything I've lost from my childhood. You must understand why you can't leave.

VIDO:

But I have to leave, Madam. I have to. Despite the danger. Despite the risks. Despite the war which is still going on.

THE MOTHER:

The war is over. It's been over for months. Finished. The peace treaty's been signed. Let there be peace and harmony for all mankind. The bad guys lost, the good guys won and the guys in the middle, that huge mass of mediocrity, are shouting victory. They're tracking down the coyotes and secretly looking forward to the next conflict. War is so handy. Every horror imaginable can be justified. Your soldier was right. You are free. There's nothing keeping you here. I'm asking you to stay. We've found our very own harmony. We're a family. I'm asking you to stay.

VIDO:

I have to leave, Madam. For my parents, my father, my mother. I have to find them. They wrote to me. I have to find them.

THE MOTHER:

They're dead. They were taken prisoner. They were separated. They were deported. They were slaughtered. At the very beginning. I have their death certificates. There were no letters. There never were. I wrote them myself, late at night, by candlelight, with my left hand so they'd look more authentic, more tortured. I enjoyed making up those letters from beyond the grave. It amused me. You should've guessed. Poor souls.

Letters don't exist where they were. There was nothing there. Nothing but death in all its forms. Death. Death. You have no one left out there. I'm asking you to stay.

VIDO:

I have to leave, Madam. Let me out of here. Let me walk in the open air, for a few hours, a few days, a few years. And then I'll come back.

THE MOTHER:

You won't. You'll leave on the back of your handsome soldier. That's what you've been waiting for. He'll make love to you. All the time. Everywhere. And because you like it, you won't come back.

VIDO:

I'll come back: I promise. You have my word, Madam, I'll come back to see you, Igor, and Jana of course. I will come back.

THE MOTHER:

You won't. You'll forget us over there on the plains of Dakota. Is that what you call gratitude, you ungrateful little slut.

VIDO:

I'm leaving, Madam. I ask one thing. One. One last favour: give me your blessing, Madam. Bless me.

THE MOTHER:

I curse you, Vido. I curse you. I put every ounce of strength I have into this curse, may it follow you, may it precede you. You're evil. You dusted our house, cleaned our dirt, became intimate with the dizzying depths of our garbage. And by doing that, you came to know the very soul of my house, you became the mistress of our consciences, our desires and our vices, and you gained great power in my home. Phenomenal power. You

control the system. You hold the keys. I have nothing left but
these knees on which to beg you: do not abandon us.

VIDO:

Get up, Madam. This isn't right.

THE MOTHER:

Don't touch me. I beg you not to go. I need you. Please. Don't do
this to me. Service. Service: the ultimate luxury. Because of you
I've acquired a taste for it. You can't leave me now.

VIDO:

Madam, please, get up. Please.

THE MOTHER:

Don't touch me. Don't leave. This is a plea, a prayer. I beg you to
hear it. I offer you the many shades of my humiliation. Here.
Help yourself. It's your turn. Take advantage of me if you want.
Abuse your power. But don't leave.

VIDO:

Don't cry, Madam. This is absurd. Madam.

THE MOTHER:

Teach me how to sweep. Tell me the names of things. The things
in my house. I no longer know the way from my bedroom to the
attic. Take my hand. I beg you. I'm lost. I'm lost.

VIDO:

Madam, don't cry. Stop acting like a child.

THE MOTHER:

Lesson number one: this is a kitchen. This is where we iron the
clothes. We wash the clothes by hand like in the old days. We
dry the clothes on strings of stars. We walk from star to star or

maybe we dance our way to heaven. Or maybe to the toilet. Or down the cesspool.

VIDO:
You're tired. Come. You'll catch cold. Come.

THE MOTHER:
Lesson number two: this is the big pot, the one for the children's bath. Big enough for one, even two. Lay black coal before lighting the fire. Use bellows to fan the flames. Simmer for an hour or two. Serve on a bed of olives and orange blossoms. Don't forget to dry the children. Afterwards.

VIDO:
I'll bring you a throw. You're freezing. Don't move.

THE MOTHER:
Lesson number three: don't confuse rags and hankies. Rags are for cleaning cobwebs. Hankies are for wiping tears and noses and also the heart when it cracks and leaks. Use to wipe the heart.

VIDO:
I'll bring you the throw. You're exhausted. I'll be back, Madam.

THE MOTHER:
Wait. You've forgotten the rats. Lesson number four: to get rid of them, take a rat poison like this one. A fast-acting rat poison. Pour it into a cup. A coffee cup. Use a generous amount. Add hot water or lemonade or maybe tea or coffee or chicory. Mix well and drink in a few short gulps.

VIDO:
I'll be back, Madam.

She exits.

THE MOTHER:

People will say all sorts of things. Times of peace are difficult.
Before, during the war, when you opened the windows colours
poured in. Those colours spoke. Of all sorts of things. They said
that if there was peace, life would be better, that the lights would
not go out anymore. Also, that a cleaning lady comes cheap and
all you have to do is want one to have one. So, in the depths of
the war, you start imagining all sorts of things: you imagine a
maid who can do everything, with smiles that are real. You
dream of order, of lavender and of watered flower gardens. And
even if it's not true, you still dream.

She drinks.

People will say all sorts of things. Times of war are easier. In the
dead of winter, you open your door to a stranger and all the
memories of childhood flood in: your brothers and sisters
shouting at play in the courtyard, your mother's orders floating
on the dust motes, the little hands that scurry about like ants.
And time. Time to laugh at nothing just because it feels so good
to laugh, time to chat about this and that, about them and us and
you and the whole world. Kitchen time, and cooking time that
went on and on and on because we had the time. The time to live.

She drinks.

People will say all sorts of things. There are no masters, there are
no slaves. There are ways of living or surviving and when you
can't face the violence of war any more, you look for what you
can, and you take what you find. And what you find is your
childhood, the vast country of your childhood. There's the
courtyard, the voices and the kitchen. And a mother who says
"Lemon" and ten little hands rush to serve her lemon. "Fountain"
and my sisters and I are deluged from our toes to our nose with

pearls of falling water. "Dreams" and we could sleep peacefully until noon because they were there, the little hands, making the coffee, the tea, the chicory.

She drinks.

People will say all sorts of things. Times don't change. There's no then and now. There's no here and there. There's no gratitude or consideration or respect. Only one thing remains: self-interest. Everything can be bought, everything can be sold, everything has a price tag. Everything. There is no humanity. There is no humanity.

She dies.

THE END

Translator's Note:

I felt that a few words about the French title of this play, *Le Complexe de Thénardier*, might be of interest.

The Thenardier complex is not an actual term used in modern psychology, like inferiority complex or Oedipus complex. It was invented by the playwright and refers to characters in *Les Misérables,* Victor Hugo's nineteenth century novel, a classic of French literature that has probably been read by every French high school student for, at the very least, the past hundred years. Suffice to say that there is a certain resonance in French that is completely lost on anglophones! I suppose an equivalent might be the Fagan complex.

I would like to elaborate a little on the reference because I think it helps us to understand the world of the play. At one point in Victor Hugo's novel, Cosette, one of the main characters in the book, is left by her mother in the care of an apparently pleasant couple, by the name of Thénardier, who run an inn. They have children of their own and agree to take her in provided her mother pays them room and board. In no time, however, Cosette becomes their servant. They exploit her mercilessly. A very complex relationship then develops between the couple and their "charge." It's a relationship that raises all sorts of questions: what is the nature of servitude? Of service? Of ownership? Who needs who more in this kind of relationship, the master or the servant? And who is the real master and who is the real "slave"? Where is the power in this kind of power-based relationship? Can it shift? Is it shared? What maintains the balance when there is one?

A few years ago, on a trip back home to Africa, José Pliya witnessed the "complexe de Thénardier" being played out between his mother and the village girls (the Vido Mingons) working in his childhood home. This became the inspiration for the play.

About the playwright:

José Pliya was born in Cotonou, Bénin, in 1966. After studying and teaching in France, he went on to head up various Alliances Françaises offices, working in Guinea, Cameroun, Dominica and Martinique where, in 2003, he founded an association of Caribbean playwrights which includes francophone, anglophone, hispanophone and Creole writers. In September 2005, he was named director of the Scène nationale de l Artchipel in Guadeloupe.

His plays include *Negrerrances, Le Masque de Sika, Une famille ordinaire, Parabole* and *Nous étions assis sur le rivage du monde* which premiered at the 2005 Festival de théâtre des Amériques (Montreal) directed by Québécois director Denis Marleau. From there, it went on to the Festival international de la Francophonie (Limoges, France) and was also presented at the National Arts Centre in Ottawa.

About the translator:

Maureen LaBonté is a dramaturge, translator and teacher.

In 2006, she was named head of the Banff playRites Colony at the Banff Centre for the Arts, after working as resident dramaturge at the Colony from 2003 until 2005. She was also Literary Manager in charge of play development at The Shaw Festival and worked at the National Theatre School of Canada from 1994 to 2001, running a pilot Directing Program and then coordinating the Playwrighting Program and Playwrights' Residency.

She has translated more than thirty Quebec plays into English. Recent translations include: *The Bookshop* by Marie-Josée Bastien, *Everybody's WELLES pour tous* by Patrice Dubois and Martin Labreque and *The Tailor's Will* by Michel Ouellette.

MATHILDE

(Mathilde)

By Véronique Olmi

Translated by Morwyn Brebner

Production information:

MATHILDE was first produced at the Théâtre du Rond-Point in Paris in the fall of 2003. It was directed by Didier Long and featured Pierre Arditi and Ariane Ascaride.

The translation of MATHILDE was workshopped and read at the Banff playRites Colony 2003 with Brian Dooley and Carmen Grant. Linda Gaboriau was translation dramaturge.

In June 2004, MATHILDE was chosen to represent the Banff playRites Colony at the National Arts Center's *On the Verge* Reading Series held during the Magnetic North Theatre Festival in Edmonton, Alberta. The reading was directed by Kelly Thornton and featured Brian Dooley (Pierre) and Sandra Nicholls (Mathilde).

The English-language premiere of MATHILDE opened in Toronto in April 2006. It was produced by Nightwood Theatre and starred Martha Burns and Tom McCamus. Kelly Thornton directed.

CHARACTERS

MATHILDE   a woman in her 40s or 50s
PIERRE   her husband, 50s

SETTING

Pierre and Mathilde's home – the apartment of a cultivated, well-off couple. It is messy as though they've just moved.

Mathilde, in a raincoat, holding her bag, stands facing Pierre. She seems tired. He looks surprised and uncomfortable.

MATHILDE:
   Here I am… *(beat)* Are you surprised?

PIERRE:
   A little.

MATHILDE:
   I had to come back one day, didn't I?

PIERRE:
   … yes…

MATHILDE:
   Weren't you expecting me?

PIERRE:
   … I'd forgotten…

MATHILDE:
   You wanted to forget.

PIERRE:
   I've lost my sense of time.

MATHILDE:
   Not like I have.

PIERRE:
... no... of course not.

A pause.

MATHILDE:
May I come in?

PIERRE:
Of course!

MATHILDE: *(looking around the apartment)*
Are you going away?

PIERRE:
No. Why?

MATHILDE:
Did someone break in?

PIERRE:
Things look messy – because I tidied.

MATHILDE:
Oh?

PIERRE:
It always looks like a disaster when you're cleaning up... Come
in...

She takes off her raincoat. He goes behind her to take it and hang it up.
She also gives him her handbag. She doesn't move, staying in exactly
the same place. A beat, like a hesitation.

PIERRE:

Do you have enough money? I mean... you might have taken...
did you take a cab?

MATHILDE:

The bus. Several buses.

PIERRE:

I wouldn't have had the strength to wait for you. At that place.

MATHILDE:

That's why you forgot.

PIERRE:

Perhaps...

MATHILDE: (*sincere*)

It's normal to be alone, in that place, and to leave alone.

PIERRE:

Wouldn't you rather sit?

MATHILDE: ·

No. I wouldn't rather.

PIERRE:

Fine... I'll sit... (*He sits and finds himself smaller and lower
than her. A pause.*) I understand that you feel disoriented...
I'm also having a hard time... keeping my bearings. I bundled
up so many things, put them in boxes. I even moved some of
the furniture – you've noticed, some of the furniture is in a
different place.

MATHILDE:

Like me.

Pierre hesitates. He doesn't know how he's supposed to take that.

PIERRE:
  Have you eaten?

MATHILDE:
  No.

PIERRE:
  Do you want something?

MATHILDE:
  No.

She takes a pack of cigarettes from her pocket and lights a cigarette.

PIERRE:
  So, the first thing you did was… come here?

MATHILDE:
  Yes.

PIERRE:
  To…? Pick things up?

MATHILDE:
  More or less.

PIERRE:
  I knew it. I thought: When she comes back… it'll be, well… to leave again. That's what prompted the boxes. I put your things in boxes.

MATHILDE:
  You mean… my personal things.

PIERRE:

All these objects – without you... It was driving me crazy... I became a compulsive organizer. I became the box king.

MATHILDE:

And if I'd decided to stay?

PIERRE:

I would have been surprised.

MATHILDE:

Why?

PIERRE:

I know how much you despise me.

MATHILDE:

How much?

PIERRE:

So much you'll take these boxes.

MATHILDE:

And what if I'd asked you to leave?

PIERRE:

Why me?

MATHILDE:

Why not?

PIERRE:

But I... I didn't... I never–

MATHILDE:

It's true: You never did anything.

PIERRE:
Of course…! *(a beat)* Your parents–

MATHILDE:
I'm going there later.

PIERRE:
No, I mean: they were–

MATHILDE:
Very nice.

PIERRE:
Yes. Very nice.

MATHILDE:
They called you often. They asked how you were.

PIERRE:
Yes.

MATHILDE:
You told them: "I'm fine. I'm doing some tidying."

PIERRE:
No. I didn't tell them that.

MATHILDE:
You told them: "I'm not fine. How could she do this to me?"

PIERRE:
Don't try to put yourself in my position.

MATHILDE:
You're right. Mine's enough.

A pause.

PIERRE:
You know, it's hard. I've lost a lot of clients...

MATHILDE:
You mean: I made you lose a lot of clients.

PIERRE:
Same result.

MATHILDE:
And it's the result that counts. Because of me you have
fewer patients.

PIERRE:
You know how people are.

MATHILDE:
No. Less and less.

PIERRE:
Well people... are always afraid that misfortune is contagious.

MATHILDE:
It IS contagious!

PIERRE:
Let's just say... It left its mark.

MATHILDE:
On me, mostly. I was marked.

PIERRE:
Anyhow, it's been hard... financially...

MATHILDE:
Of course. You invested in that new CT scanner...

PIERRE:
Not that that's the main thing.

MATHILDE:
Nevertheless it's what you mention.

PIERRE:
I'm doing what I can.

MATHILDE:
That's very kind.

PIERRE:
Don't mock me.

MATHILDE:
I'm not mocking you... I understand. My absence–

PIERRE:
Your actions, mostly!

MATHILDE:
Oh yes! My actions, mostly!

PIERRE:
Please!

MATHILDE:
Yes, let's put things in perspective: my actions, mostly.

PIERRE:
Please... everyone...

MATHILDE: *(over him)*
"Is responsible for his actions, my dear Mathilde."

PIERRE:
I'm not calling you "my dear Mathilde."

MATHILDE:
But you have.

PIERRE:
Under other circumstances.

MATHILDE:
Yes. In a different tone – a murmur: "my dear Mathilde."

PIERRE:
I would prefer not to talk about it.

MATHILDE:
Oh! You "would prefer"! You express yourself so well, so politely… as though I were a colleague, or a patient, even.

PIERRE:
How would you like me to speak to you?

MATHILDE:
As though I were your wife?

PIERRE:
No.

MATHILDE:
Aren't we still married?

PIERRE:
We're married. Legally.

MATHILDE:
Legally. The perfect word for me.

PIERRE:
But we're no longer husband and wife.

MATHILDE:
Very subtle. Congratulations.

PIERRE:
You've become... so cold.

MATHILDE:
It's true.

PIERRE:
Why?

MATHILDE:
Probably because I feel cold.

PIERRE:
Do you want a sweater?

MATHILDE:
If I want a sweater I'll get it. Right?

PIERRE:
Wrong.

MATHILDE:
Oh. My clothes too.

PIERRE:
I needed space.

MATHILDE:

I can just see you! Sniffing my dresses before stuffing them in a box you got from the supermarket!

PIERRE:

Do you want one of my sweaters?

MATHILDE:

No. You do that when you're in love – and naked.

PIERRE:

Why do you complain of the cold if you don't want anything?

MATHILDE:

I'm not complaining. Cold and I are good friends now. That's how it is.

PIERRE:

I'm suffocating. Maybe it's because… I'm always fussing with the apartment – I even repainted the closet.

MATHILDE:

Are you telling me… you painted the inside of a closet?

PIERRE:

So?

MATHILDE:

Nothing… It's… I didn't know you were so meticulous.

PIERRE:

There's nothing abnormal in wanting things to be neat.

MATHILDE absorbs this. A pause.

MATHILDE:
You're so tense.

PIERRE:
You've caught me unprepared... I'm kind of at a loss.

MATHILDE:
Are you expecting someone? Would you like me to leave right now?

PIERRE:
I'm not expecting anyone. Are you sure you won't sit? You seem so high up, like that... you look taller.

MATHILDE:
I think I've developed a stoop. Don't you think so?

PIERRE:
You're not stooping. You've lost weight, it's to be expected.

MATHILDE:
Why?

PIERRE:
I mean... it's understandable. Are you taking... Surely... You'd tell me if you needed a prescription?

MATHILDE:
Why would you want to stop being my husband, and become my doctor?

PIERRE:
I won't let you fall apart.

MATHILDE:
Am I going to fall apart?

PIERRE:
  I know you, you're delicate.

MATHILDE:
  Oh?

PIERRE:
  That's why you're cold.

MATHILDE:
  I'm cold because I just spent three months in a refrigerator.

PIERRE:
  I'd still prefer not to talk about that place.

MATHILDE:
  "That place" is called a detention centre. Everything is
  detained there.

PIERRE:
  Well things have been detained here too. It's been hard for
  me too.

MATHILDE:
  But you're not cold.

PIERRE:
  I'm taking medication. I'm not feeling very well.

MATHILDE:
  Not feeling very well and innocent. Innocent and victimized.

A pause.

PIERRE:
  Your parents–

MATHILDE:
You already told me that.

PIERRE:
True.

MATHILDE:
It's too bad we don't have children – they would have filled
the space.

PIERRE:
You'll see the boxes… I still haven't taken all the books down
from the shelves… I don't know anymore: yours, mine, the ones
we bought together. The ones we gave each other. The
ones you wrote. (a beat) I re-read them, you know… I find
them unbearable.

MATHILDE:
Oh! You reread them in light of my crime.

PIERRE:
In light of your actions.

MATHILDE:
Yes, that's a better phrase. More theatrical.

PIERRE:
They illuminated aspects of you I thought I knew.

MATHILDE:
They're just work. Not public psychoanalysis.

PIERRE:
Offered up to the public. Meant for them.

MATHILDE:

Not meant for. Written for. It's not the same.

PIERRE:

If only you knew how little I gave a damn… I wanted to burn down the bookshelves.

MATHILDE:

But you didn't do it. You didn't dare. Take action.

PIERRE:

I don't give a damn about any of it. You can take whatever you want.

MATHILDE:

Do you think that's why I came back?

PIERRE:

I don't think anything.

MATHILDE:

What do you think I came for? My car, my books… You?

PIERRE:

I loved you so much…

MATHILDE:

Ha! And is there anything left?

PIERRE:

Inevitably.

MATHILDE:

You're not someone who can love spontaneously. Out of time. No. It's more… settled. There's always something left.

PIERRE:

You think that's wrong?

MATHILDE:

I admire you. Able to live tepidly. Not cold. Not hot. Just tepid. Always a little left. At the bottom of the cup.

PIERRE:

You've always found other people's pain insipid.

MATHILDE:

That's not true.

PIERRE:

Small. Petty. You like to cut to the quick. Things have to be gory, you want to get your money's worth.

MATHILDE:

My money?

PIERRE:

You earn plenty for your pain. You recycle it into paperbacks.

MATHILDE:

Oh that's nice. Ever the lover of literature. I don't like your bitterness. Your mouth must reek from saying what you just said.

PIERRE:

Do I disgust you?

MATHILDE:

No, I'm too cold. Too removed…

PIERRE:

Stop standing like that… Like you're visiting.

MATHILDE:

I am visiting. You're going to give me the boxes and I'm going to leave.

PIERRE:

Where will you live?

MATHILDE:

That's a good one… What will become of her? With whom will she live? What medication will she require?

PIERRE:

Does it weigh on you that I still love you?

MATHILDE:

What weighed on me was three months – without one visit. One letter.

PIERRE:

I know you, I knew your pride couldn't have stood it.

MATHILDE:

My pride? What were you thinking?

PIERRE:

Nothing.

MATHILDE:

What did you pretend? Did you convince yourself I was at the spa? On a book tour?

PIERRE:

I didn't pretend anything!

MATHILDE:
It humiliates you, doesn't it, that your wife did time? So, in order to bear it, you convince yourself you still love her a little, and it all becomes "painfully romantic." (*A pause.*) If you don't want to know what I went through there, don't ask me how I'll live here.

PIERRE:
Mathilde... After what happened, it was too hard for me to go.

MATHILDE goes to him, squats to his level. Pierre is uncomfortable, disturbed by the proximity.

MATHILDE: (*slowly*)
What happened, Pierre?

PIERRE:
... your actions...

MATHILDE:
What actions?

PIERRE:
Mathilde!

MATHILDE:
What actions? I want you to tell me. In your own words. Not ones from the trial, or the papers. What happened?

PIERRE:
What you did to me–

MATHILDE: (*interrupting*)
No! Not did TO YOU. DID.

PIERRE:
You cheated… No! You cheated ON ME! You cheated on me
with a kid!

MATHILDE:
And?

PIERRE:
And it hurt.

MATHILDE:
Where?

PIERRE:
What do you mean, "where"?

MATHILDE:
Where did it hurt?

A beat.

PIERRE:
Everywhere.

She stands.

MATHILDE:
That's too vast. I don't believe it.

PIERRE:
I had to reconsider my whole life. My life with you.

MATHILDE:
Because I held a young man of fifteen in my arms?

PIERRE:
Yes.

MATHILDE:
You mean your life was that tenuous? Was it so delicate that my
arms wrapped around someone else could devastate and hurt
you? Everywhere at once?

PIERRE:
I trusted you.

MATHILDE:
Trusted what, in me?

PIERRE:
Just... trust.

MATHILDE:
I don't understand. Trust in my eyes, that cheated on you if they
looked at someone else? Trust in my hands, that cheated on you
if they touched any skin but yours? Trust in my desire that hurt
you when it satisfied itself with someone else? It's not natural.

PIERRE:
Some people call it love.

MATHILDE:
I pity them.

PIERRE:
I think you'd better leave.

MATHILDE:
I think I'd better understand, before I leave.

PIERRE:

These are things you feel physically. That pass through your body. Yes, maybe it felt good to you, but to us – for the rest of us, it hurt.

MATHILDE:

Oh, no! It was good for all of you too. Now you all know why you're in pain, you, our parents and our so-called friends: it's Mathilde's fault. Because Mathilde fucked – yes, there's no other word, imagine, even at the trial she said it wasn't for love, it was for pleasure, that's what she said! Love! That's all right – there's always something left, but pleasure? What's left? It was good for all of you. Come on, there was solidarity, support! I'm sure my mother finally had the pleasure (oh my God!), the satisfaction of being examined by you, and that you prescribed her some mild antidepressants, telling her how remarkable she was. Everyone knows families get along better when there's a sick child.

PIERRE:

And you? It was good for you too. All those people who stood up for you! The intelligentsia to the rescue of Mathilde Esnault, their new cause. How many important people signed that petition?

MATHILDE:

I don't know… I've forgotten.

PIERRE:

One had to do it. Like going to opening night at the Opera - the mandatory petition!

MATHILDE:

You always said writers were selfish. You were mistaken.

MATHILDE   237

PIERRE:
I wonder why they signed... for you or for them... What do you think?

MATHILDE:
Nothing. All I know is it was comforting while I was alone and that's a lot.

PIERRE:
I was alone too. And close to you... (a beat) I lay in our bed at night, thinking of you. Every night. I prayed – to whom I don't know, but I prayed, for someone, something, to enfold you, protect you.

MATHILDE:
Protect me from what? You don't answer. You're allowed not to. During the whole thing, I wasn't allowed to ask any questions... I was the one who gave answers – correct answers.

PIERRE:
Yes, you were the defendant.

MATHILDE:
The whole thing was so private... everything I had to say was so personal...

PIERRE:
You had to pay your debt... to society, to that kid's parents.

MATHILDE:
That "kid," as you call him, had had other lovers, and his parents weren't expecting anything, they were so sure of everything and so full of hate!

A beat.

PIERRE:

But who would you ask questions to?

MATHILDE:

My accusers, naturally. Find out what they do with their desire, their turmoil, their doubt…

PIERRE: (*interrupting*)

Corrupting a minor is an illegal act, what followed was purely logical.

MATHILDE:

But since desire isn't logical, how can you logically shut someone away for his desire? Don't sensuality and beauty amaze you too? Tell me. Tell me what devastates you.

PIERRE:

I'm not the defendant.

MATHILDE:

I'm not accusing you. I'm asking what overwhelms you.

PIERRE:

I know how to control my impulses.

MATHILDE:

Oh… poor things…

PIERRE:

I master them.

MATHILDE:

Haven't you ever lost it?

PIERRE:

I didn't say it was easy.

MATHILDE:
I understand why I needed that affair...

PIERRE:
When I found out what you'd done, I was lost.

MATHILDE:
Did that feel good?

PIERRE:
It hurt me. And I'm not masochistic.

MATHILDE:
Oh Pierre! Please! Tell me you can be overwhelmed, that you'd be capable of it.

PIERRE:
The things that get to me are ordinary, concrete. Certainly not impossible or forbidden.

MATHILDE:
Such as?

PIERRE:
I don't know... tiny things... subtle...

MATHILDE:
Tell me about them.

PIERRE:
Well... when I sorted your things, I found – mixed in with everything – I found the little notes we used to scribble to each other, when we'd go out.

MATHILDE:
And?

PIERRE:

And it was ridiculous... They were moving.

MATHILDE:

What else?

PIERRE:

Nothing... they were... We'd written things like "If Lena calls tell her the meeting's still on," "Don't forget the dry cleaning," "I'll be home late, there are eggs in the fridge."

MATHILDE:

It's sweet... a tad maternal – nothing more.

PIERRE:

I'm sure you could read an entire life into those words, left on the table, on the bed, by the phone. Do you remember the time you wrote in lipstick on the bathroom mirror?

MATHILDE:

No.

PIERRE:

Like a fool, I cleaned it up!

MATHILDE:

What did I write?

PIERRE:

I don't know anymore. It doesn't matter.

MATHILDE:

What does? Matter?

PIERRE:

The attention we pay each other, the special little things you do… Words that mean: "take care of yourself."

MATHILDE:

What if I'd written: "There are eggs in the fridge. Don't wait for me to eat, tonight I'm taking care of MYSELF"?

PIERRE:

On those nights you didn't care what there was to eat… And you didn't write.

MATHILDE:

The same thing could have happened to you.

PIERRE:

Sometimes I desire women, but I don't for a second think of ruining my life for a moment of pleasure.

MATHILDE:

You're right. Why ruin your life? Why not decide that instead of being dirty it's respectable. Respectable and necessary.

PIERRE:

Because I'm a moron who's faithful to his wife.

MATHILDE:

Faithful to an idea. But your desires are full of other women. You've wanted women you passed in the street, while we were walking side-by-side, you've wanted actresses, while we were holding hands at the movies, maybe you even thought of them again, later, when we had sex. We're seldom alone when we make love.

PIERRE:

This is a rather limited conversation. I can see it coming - you'll review my life and end up asking me... if I ever got a hard-on telling a pretty girl she had breast cancer!

MATHILDE:

Really? That... I wouldn't have imagined... Does that happen?

PIERRE:

You can twist it a million ways but the fact remains: you betrayed me while there was a bond between us, real trust.

MATHILDE:

An ongoing hypocrisy. If you think I regret what happened, oh no! I liked fucking that boy too much.

PIERRE:

That's enough.

MATHILDE:

I liked his smell, his hands, his ass, his chest, I liked him down to the roots of his hair and his gums–

PIERRE:

I told you that's enough!

MATHILDE:

What would you have wanted? For me to fall in love with him? Plan a future with him? Would you have preferred that it be serious instead of light?

PIERRE:

I would have preferred that it didn't exist! That you'd never met him, goddamit! Do you know many guys who like their wives screwing fifteen-year-old boys?

MATHILDE:
I don't know a lot of "guys."

PIERRE:
One is enough, eh? Did you think you were Pygmalion?

MATHILDE:
He didn't need me to instruct him.

PIERRE:
He admitted you were his first… "mature woman."

MATHILDE:
Did you want to say: "old woman"?

PIERRE:
Compared to him, yes. Until all this happened, I hadn't noticed how far we were from childhood. How the generations had come up behind us, without our noticing.

MATHILDE:
It's the normal cycle of life.

PIERRE:
In the normal cycle of life you would have a fifteen-year-old, not be the mistress of one.

MATHILDE:
One wouldn't have precluded the other.

PIERRE:
A child would have grounded you.

MATHILDE:
That's probably why I didn't want any. So I could lift off.

PIERRE: *(ironic)*
Yes, probably…

MATHILDE:
I wasn't in that boy's arms to taste the pleasures of incest.

PIERRE:
Who knows?

MATHILDE:
But maybe that would make it easier for you? If there was an explanation. A word for it. How simple that world view must be. Yes, he was fifteen and I'm nearly fifty. So? It was now or never.

PIERRE:
But I'm here. To be with you. Grow old with you.

MATHILDE:
United by the sacred bonds of time and marriage! And if I'm overcome with desire again, you'll be there to yell incest? Pedophilia? Everyone must stay with their double, their other half - grow old together, end up looking like each other, until you can't tell husband and wife from brother and sister… Is that healthier?

PIERRE:
It's the natural order of things.

MATHILDE:
I don't like order.

PIERRE:
You will! There's a time for everything. And whether you like it or not, you'll age. Sleeping with a kid is just an exotic treat, not a face lift. You age, you become wise, and pleasure yields to tenderness.

MATHILDE:
Oh no! Don't kill me with tenderness! That half-measure we call to the rescue when we can't get it up! I renounce it! Tenderness and everything touching. You and me, old folks without children, walking hand in hand down the sidewalk to the park! Tenderness is what you give when there's nothing left and I still want everything that shines, that bangs, that howls!

PIERRE:
Did you need a teenager for that?

MATHILDE:
Who knows? Someone unmarked. Light. Who didn't carry the worries of the world on his shoulders, who thought the world was new and he was at its centre. Someone with no past who thought Marx was the name of a toy gorilla and that Chechnya was a folk dance – why are you laughing? That's how things should be: easy and flowing.

PIERRE:
It really didn't have much of a future...

MATHILDE:
He was as refreshing as water from a spring.

PIERRE:
You would have tired of him, I know you. And what was this innocent youth doing in a writing workshop?

MATHILDE:
He came to meet me.

PIERRE:

You're being completely dishonest! I can imagine him, driving to the rendezvous on his moped and you… waiting for him in the room, fixing your stockings, powdering your nose again and trying to convince him you liked the lights low!

MATHILDE:

I do like the lights low. I write and I fuck with the lights low.

PIERRE:

And that pimply, badlyshaven little stud who must have taken such pride in being your last chance!

MATHILDE:

How long did you steep in hate to come up with that?

PIERRE:

I have no hate. I've just opened my eyes.

MATHILDE:

Close them and stop thinking of me with that boy. I guarantee you've got it wrong.

PIERRE:

It's worse with my eyes closed.

MATHILDE:

Was it you in that boy's arms? Or me?

PIERRE:

Maybe me even more than you… I wanted to go blow up all the high schools, burn down the discos, impose a martial law that would forbid teenagers to leave the house after six pm…. and when I passed one in the street… Oh! The way they all laugh! Awkward, insecure, and yet the arrogance!

MATHILDE:
You shouldn't have had to suffer for every teenager you met – I only had one.

PIERRE:
It's like you had them all. All the ones to come, too.

MATHILDE:
Listen, a moment of pleasure is nothing... a gust of fresh air, a breath of poetry – do you own my breath?

PIERRE:
I didn't find being alone with a TV tray, waiting for you while you were with him, very poetic.

MATHILDE:
You didn't know I was with him.

PIERRE:
I knew I was alone.

MATHILDE:
You never noticed his smell on me when I got home – that made me angry... that you didn't feel how full I was of him, how he had permeated my body.

PIERRE:
You headed right for the shower.

MATHILDE:
Yes. Even though I wanted to save it... But there was always a little, left on my fingers.

PIERRE:
You came straight here... to tell me all this?

MATHILDE:

No. But being here… in this apartment, full of my history, my secrets–

PIERRE:

It's not the apartment, it's me - seeing the husband makes you think of the lover. It happens all the time now. I'm getting used to it.

MATHILDE:

I come back… We speak… and everything becomes terrible…

PIERRE:

And… and… Must you stand there…? Like a passer-by?

MATHILDE: (laughs)

Is that what this is all about?

PIERRE:

Look, it bothers me… it's irritating… it's like we're still in court – that's why we can't talk about anything else, the way you're standing is so "court of law"…

MATHILDE sits.

MATHILDE:

There.

PIERRE:

… that's better. Isn't it?

MATHILDE:

I don't want us to yell anymore.

PIERRE:
All right... we'll just whine...

A pause.

MATHILDE:
Is it true that every night I was in that place... you slept alone
every night?

PIERRE:
It may seem incredible to you, but yes.

MATHILDE:
Did you think of me? Did it give you pleasure?

PIERRE:
Sometimes... sometimes pleasure... sometimes disgust.

MATHILDE:
Pleasure and disgust are linked. Pleasure and loneliness, too.
Pleasure goes with everything. That's why we never get enough
of it. How did you think of me? With whom?

PIERRE:
I was thinking of what I like – liked, in you... that way you had
of... *(a beat)* I love you, even if it's not what you want.

MATHILDE:
There's something unfair about your love.

PIERRE:
It's called "jealousy". *(A beat. Mathilde seems unwell.)* Mathilde?

MATHILDE:
Get me a glass of water.

PIERRE:
Water? Just water?

MATHILDE:
Yes. Just water.

PIERRE:
How about tea?

MATHILDE:
Clean transparent water in a clean transparent glass.

A pause. He brings her a drink.

PIERRE:
Will that do? Are you sure? *(she signals yes)* You should lie down
a moment.

MATHILDE:
I'm used to it. It'll pass. *(She drinks. A beat.)* So… so you lost a
lot of clients.

PIERRE:
Yes. I became suspect… At first, I thought there was… people
would drop by for no reason – almost no reason… I thought
there was a burst of solidarity. It's when they stopped coming
that I understood.

MATHILDE:
Understood what?

PIERRE:
One time a patient asked me if I still had your picture on my
desk. I said: "How do you know I have a picture of my wife on
my desk?" She said: "I didn't know. I just took a stab at it." That's

what they were doing, inventing minor pains and passing
illnesses - taking a stab.

MATHILDE:

Isn't it terrible being at the mercy of others? All the idiots our
lives depend on?

PIERRE:

I depended on them, and I didn't even know it. Then one day,
nobody – not you, not them, nobody needed me.

MATHILDE:

We weren't bound to each other.

PIERRE:

You were my life, you and my patients. (beat.) I stay in now,
most of the time... I tidy... I file... I think... of the patients who
placed their hope in me and how I always hesitated, knowing
how painful the truth is.

MATHILDE:

You said some wanted to hear it.

PIERRE:

A lot of them gave up when I told them their prognosis.

MATHILDE:

But not all.

PIERRE:

No. Some of them finally had a goal in life - staying alive, for the
first time. I lost my clients. Dying without me, the undesirable
doctor. Until then I'd never understood to what extent I was
your husband, and that for everyone, I'd stopped being the
writer's husband and become the scandalous writer's husband.

MATHILDE:
I was judged scandalous because I was a writer. I wouldn't have had to pay such a price for corrupting a minor if I had been less famous.

PIERRE:
Maybe, but it has its advantages - your publisher told me sales were up. Before the trial you were famous. Today you're a celebrity.

MATHILDE:
Possibly.

PIERRE:
I imagine you've had lots of offers. Your story will be worth a lot.

MATHILDE:
I didn't write in prison.

PIERRE:
You'll write here.

MATHILDE:
I can't.

PIERRE:
It'll come.

MATHILDE:
No.

PIERRE:
It'll come, I'm telling you. (*a beat*) I read the press files – well, the newspapers… There was an interview with that… boy… that guy… your student… he was certainly chattier than at the trial! Anyway… It wasn't exactly a love story!

MATHILDE:

Are you sorry?

PIERRE:

It would have been more forgivable.

MATHILDE:

I don't need to be forgiven. Don't need to justify myself. To talk about it. To write.

PIERRE:

You just got out. Wait a little. I give you two weeks.

MATHILDE:

They gave me three months and you give me two weeks. Why do you all get to decide about my time?

PIERRE:

You did a good job of ruining ours.

MATHILDE:

I didn't ask you all to get involved in my affairs!

PIERRE:

You always involve us in yours! The way you romanticize the world's pain!

MATHILDE:

I never write about the world's pain.

PIERRE:

You're right. You romanticize your navel, that's what you do. To hide your hand you change the names and the timelines, but it's the same deal.

MATHILDE:

You're the one who romanticizes the world, getting a hard-on telling someone they have breast cancer.

PIERRE:

That never happened, I imagined it happening.

MATHILDE:

You certainly have a fertile imagination. Once – no, more than once – you told me it excited you to imagine me in another man's arms.

PIERRE:

It was a kind of... declaration of love.

MATHILDE:

Just saying it excited you.

PIERRE:

It was a fantasy. I could have watched.

MATHILDE:

And if you watch, I'm not cheating on you? Is that it? And what would I have been allowed to do with that man? Huh? How far would you have let me go?

PIERRE:

Sleeping with that boy without telling me was giving your word then going back on it!

MATHILDE:

And if I'd asked your permission would you have given it? Liar! Anyway since doing it made me feel better, maybe it was good for both of us, and he's the one who was cheated on, but he didn't give a damn, he was free!

PIERRE:

Not free. Indifferent.

MATHILDE:

Whereas you're especially attached to me? I'm reserved for you?
Like a good table at a restaurant?

PIERRE:

You're my wife.

MATHILDE:

"My wife – Mathilde…" Until I couldn't stand it! "I'd like you
to meet my wife – Mathilde!" Why did we have to go out
every night?

PIERRE:

It's called a "social life" and at the time it didn't bother you.
You'd spend hours in the bathroom before we left.

MATHILDE:

It was so important to you that I was sexy! Sure it took time:
make-up, jewelry, tight skirts and high heels. It wasn't exactly
comfortable.

PIERRE:

That's what you say now, but at the time you loved it when
people thought you looked attractive, you flirted to cover up
your wrinkles, you asked the surgeons' wives for advice. There
was something provincial about it–

MATHILDE:

That made you laugh?

PIERRE:
  No. It was touching and bizarrely... young.

He's moved. He leaves the room. She's alone. We see her exhaustion, her internal tension. She's cold. Pierre returns with two boxes which he places at her feet. He leaves, returns with two more, places them at her feet too.

PIERRE:
  These are yours... If you'd prefer, I'll take them to you... wherever you go.

MATHILDE:
  Wherever I go...

A beat.

PIERRE:
  Before you leave, maybe we should... We should stop talking and just touch each other, huh? Just touch...?

Beat. She looks at him. She rises slowly to him. They face each other. Gently, carefully, she runs her fingers along his cheek. He trembles with emotion, suddenly backs away.

PIERRE:
  I'm sorry...

MATHILDE:
  What you just did... being on the verge of tears... That's why I fell in love with you.

PIERRE:
  I'm better. It's passed...

MATHILDE:
The first time I saw you cry was in that little church. I barely knew you. We were listening to a string quartet. The cello made you cry. Remember that? It touched me... no. It attracted me. That's what attracted me.

PIERRE:
The cello didn't make me cry.

MATHILDE:
No?

PIERRE:
No. I cried because I was in love with you.

MATHILDE:
But we didn't know each other! We'd just met, remember, you were just finishing your residency.

PIERRE:
I'm telling you the cello didn't make me cry.

MATHILDE:
Too bad.

PIERRE:
If you have to take the boxes, take them soon. I can't stand them. They're like little coffins.

MATHILDE:
I don't want them. There's only one thing I want.

PIERRE:
What?

MATHILDE:

The stones I gathered when we went hiking. They were old.
I might have been the first person to touch them. They're better
than pictures for remembering a trip, don't you think? A white
stone from Mount Ventoux, a red stone from Esterel, a fossil
from Dakar...

PIERRE:

Yes... they're much better than pictures...

MATHILDE:

Looking at them doesn't make you feel old, you don't say, "My
god! I was so foolish then, look at my haircut and that dress I
had on!" No, you touch the stone and you feel the same shapes,
the same sensations.

She looks at the boxes.

"Diskettes and miscellaneous papers" that one must have taken
some time. I'm sure you read them, my day books in particular.
Are they in there? That's what the betrayed husband, as you
would say, reads first. That... detective side is logical.

PIERRE:

Have I really become a monster?

MATHILDE:

No. You don't hold your head so high now. The day of my trial
you seemed so sure of yourself... and I heard you, you said – I
can't remember if it was to a lawyer or a reporter - you said: "I'll
be strong..."

PIERRE: *(interrupting)*

I had to be to see our private life dragged out in court! I don't
know if you remember, but they asked me if I satisfied you, how

often we had relations, it was humiliating, appalling... and that judge who wouldn't believe I hadn't noticed anything! He thought I was ridiculous... that's what I became at the trial: a ridiculous man...

MATHILDE:

Everyone respected you - your bearing, your composure... you were really... exemplary, bravely facing things and that's how you were later when you went through my papers - the brave husband, bravely searching his wife's day book for the dates and times of her meetings with her lover. But what you don't know is that those meetings were less important than the moment when I wrote down the time and date, because from that moment on, I prepared, I planned, and that time lasted infinitely longer than the meeting itself, private time that belonged to me and me alone.

A beat. She looks at a box. Reads "Warm clothing."
She opens it, takes out a sweater, puts it on.

PIERRE:

If you leave, I'll throw it all out. I'll give you the stones and throw it all out.

MATHILDE:

Good.

PIERRE:

I'll sell the apartment too.

MATHILDE:

Don't.

PIERRE:

Why not?

MATHILDE:

I don't know... The day... Do you remember the day I moved in?

PIERRE: (smiling)

Oh my god!

MATHILDE:

As though I was bringing my whole life with me.

PIERRE:

It's true, you took up a lot of space.

MATHILDE:

I'd had my suitcases packed for quite a while. I wanted so badly for you to ask me to come. You weren't expecting the two cats. And the dog. Admit it.

PIERRE:

You never arrive empty-handed.

MATHILDE:

Admit it, at first you were kind of disappointed That first night... the dog barking like crazy outside our door... you had some regrets...?

PIERRE:

On the contrary. I would have wanted the whole world to bark outside our door. I'd have told them: "Bark! Bark away! You'll never see so much as my wife's ankle!"

MATHILDE: (she laughs)

You're the mutt.

PIERRE:

Listen, I have an idea! I've been thinking since... well, since before the whole thing happened... It's been so long since... What do you say we... Throw ourselves into a project, finally make, you know, our dream come true... The house, by the sea. We could look for it together. And if you wanted we could even live there. Year-round. What do you say?

MATHILDE:

It's too big.

PIERRE:

What?

MATHILDE:

The sea. Too powerful. I need ordinary things that won't pressure me... a gentle re-entry into life... You know, the way you open your eyes a little in the morning and then close them. Wait. Look at the room again, eyes half-closed. Close them again... (*She stifles a sob.*) I haven't talked this much in months.

PIERRE:

I understand.

MATHILDE:

All I want is to breathe. Without feeling sick. To stop remembering. To stop thinking about the last few months. (*beat.*) Unless... Do you want to know?

PIERRE:

No.

MATHILDE:

It's true it would be a little late.

PIERRE:

I look at you and I can tell.

MATHILDE:

You can't tell anything. You just know that something's come undone and that, tonight, nothing in the world would make you take me out to dinner. Now you couldn't introduce me as "my wife – Mathilde" without blushing. Am I wrong?

PIERRE:

It's true. You've changed.

MATHILDE:

Too bad! I suited you so well! The perfect accessory for the well-to-do oncologist made for a life of science and fun…

PIERRE:

I was proud to have you on my arm.

MATHILDE:

We smiled a lot but at whom? Other people or the mirror?

PIERRE:

At life, perhaps.

MATHILDE:

Certainly not! The conversation was always about terminal phases, protocols, euthanasia – maybe you've broken the law too?

PIERRE:

Never.

MATHILDE:

So to stay on the right side of the law, you let people suffer?

PIERRE:

That's none of your business! You have no idea what torture it is! Do you know what it's like to wake up every day wondering: "Will I see someone die today?" No! What you wonder is: "Will I be inspired? Ah! If not, I'll write some letters!" Your only reality is fiction. My reality is sickness and death. So no, it's none of your business...

A beat.

MATHILDE:

So, we were always alone... Together and alone.

A beat.

PIERRE:

You know, I can always start looking for the house by the sea. What do you say? Then when... when your eyes are wide open... you'll come...

MATHILDE:

What's the point. You'll always feel that disgust for what I did. That blame.

PIERRE:

That depends on you.

MATHILDE:

On me?

PIERRE:

Maybe with time you'll look at the whole thing the way you look at an old photo? Finding yourself foolish and old-fashioned.

MATHILDE:
  You're vile!

PIERRE:
  I'm vile? Do you know why I flinched when you touched my
  cheek? Because your fingers are ice cold! Because you're cold,
  loveless, empty!

MATHILDE:
  Don't shout!

PIERRE:
  It's my house and I'll yell if I want to yell! And I was definitely
  wrong, we shouldn't touch each other. We should punch each
  other in the face. I can't breathe either! I'm suffocating too!

MATHILDE:
  So middle class…

PIERRE:
  Until recently you enjoyed being middle class, didn't you? An
  easy life, your head in the clouds. (imitating her.) "Oh I'm way
  too absent-minded, my husband takes care of everything at
  home." The old idiot with his housekeeping and his middle-class
  dreams of tenderness and a cottage by the sea!

MATHILDE:
  I can't go to the seaside with a man with such a hateful little face!

PIERRE:
  Then why did you come here, huh? Why? Answer me, for
  Christ's sake!

MATHILDE:

I don't want to answer you. I don't want to talk to you anymore.
I hate you.

PIERRE:

You hate me because I make you uncomfortable. I know you
too well. The fairytale about the delicate, suffering woman
doesn't work on me. I know who you are: a driven woman.
And terribly selfish.

MATHILDE:

Selfish? I spent my life waiting for you. When you came home
late. When you left again on weekends. When you were on duty
for the holidays and when I wasn't waiting, I was accompanying
you to dinner parties that were a foretaste of death itself!

PIERRE:

You're lying! It's frightening how you lie! In Amsterdam, for
instance! In Amsterdam, the night of our wedding anniversary,
good God, have you forgotten? We... We were sort of taking
stock and you said: "I like it when people need you because you
leave, but you always come back to me."

MATHILDE:

Shut up. It's vile to dig up good memories! To rub my nose in
them! I want nothing to do with it.

A pause.

PIERRE:

I'm going to order something in. Would you rather have pizza
or Chinese?

MATHILDE:

I'm telling you I'm not hungry. Where are my car keys?

PIERRE:

In your car, no doubt. You know me... leaving the keys in the ignition, no worries about theft – I have no sense of property. *(MATHILDE lets out a little, almost sad, laugh. She lights a cigarette.)* I'm funny, aren't I.

MATHILDE:

I understand you want us to separate on good terms, but I have to go now, I'm exhausted.

PIERRE:

You came... right here... You put on that sweater... and in that sweater... smoking... with that faraway look, you're like you used to be – thinking about a new novel... or what you just finished writing... *(MATHILDE smiles at him.)* ... you say: "Pierre... can I read you what I wrote today? I think there's something there... I think... tell me." *(A beat. MATHILDE is really listening.)* In Biarritz once, do you remember? It was raining, and we were having coffee in that... that... ancient tea room – do you remember Biarritz?

MATHILDE:

I remember.

PIERRE:

There were all these old women eating cake and drinking tea, you told me the life stories of these women you didn't know, it made us laugh at first, you were mean, making fun of the frightening way their dentures clicked against the custard tarts, and their smudged lipstick... that's right, at first you made fun of them, then...

A beat.

MATHILDE:
I remember.

PIERRE:
Then suddenly we felt close to those old women.

MATHILDE:
All of a sudden we loved them.

PIERRE:
And you wrote their story on a paper napkin – you reminded me
of a painter.

MATHILDE:
The next day it was nice out and we forgot about it.

PIERRE:
The next day we went swimming.

MATHILDE:
It wasn't a swim, it was a feat.

PIERRE:
Weren't we the only ones? Really the only ones!

MATHILDE:
Why are you talking to me about Biarritz?

She grabs her stomach.

PIERRE:
Is it your stomach?

MATHILDE:
Yes.

PIERRE:
Do you have anything with you?

MATHILDE:
No.

PIERRE:
I'll write you a prescription for Mylanta, it's the best. You should
eat something instead of smoking.

MATHILDE:
Do you think Mylanta is better than Maalox? In that place, they
gave me Maalox.

PIERRE:
Were you afraid at night, in that place?

MATHILDE:
I thought you'd rather not talk about it?

PIERRE:
That's what I prayed for at night - that you would be protected
while you slept. What were you afraid of?

A beat.

MATHILDE:
Of the others' lives.

PIERRE:
The others?

MATHILDE:
Yes, I was afraid of those women's lives. I couldn't bear to hear their stories. They fascinated me and they horrified me and I wondered why... why my own life is so clean – so protected. (*a beat*) You know, when you discover a world that seemed so remote, and when you enter that world that seemed so abstract and so... meant for others, then you feel like we're all part of the same species, a species just trying to survive. I know now, with such clarity, that I'm going to die. It's as inescapable as crossing the threshold of a cell and hearing... (*a beat*) the key turn in the lock. (*a beat*) I dreamed of you, in that place.

PIERRE:
Really?

MATHILDE:
You were different – physically. You weren't the same.

PIERRE:
What was I like?

MATHILDE: (*little smile*)
Fat. Very, very fat.

PIERRE:
My God!

MATHILDE:
But I loved it. It was reassuring. I dreamed you lay down on top of me and it was like... like I was holding a huge stuffed toy in my arms.

PIERRE: (*laughs*)
Fat and hairy! (*a little worried*) Would you like me... fat and hairy?

MATHILDE:
You had a beard when we met.

PIERRE:
So I'd look older – patients always mistook me for a student. The chief of staff told me the beard would reassure them.

MATHILDE:
See! Hair inspires confidence.

They look at each other, amused.

PIERRE:
You always said being with a bearded man is like making love on a rug.

MATHILDE:
Me? I said that? No!

PIERRE:
Yeah, yeah, I remember! That's why I shaved it off. (*a beat*) If you want, I could gain weight…

MATHILDE:
Why?

PIERRE:
To… To lie on top of you…

MATHILDE:
If you lay on top of me, I'd still be cold.

PIERRE:
I could lie on top of you while you slept, while you were dreaming…?

MATHILDE:
Please…

PIERRE:
If you leave me, what will I do with everything I know about you? Mathilde, we're bound to each other, linked, attached… I know so many things, I've learned them, day after day, I have them here… deep within me, under my skin!

MATHILDE:
They're called "memories," Pierre. Everyone has them. Everyone lives with them.

PIERRE:
You're not really here! You can't really belong to me if you're absent from yourself. That's why, do you understand? Do you hear what I'm saying? (a beat) I know how you can get over it, I've always known what was good for you. You need to write.

MATHILDE:
"Write"! You can't write on command! I can't. I'm out of cigarettes.

PIERRE:
I still don't smoke.

MATHILDE:
You didn't find any packs when you sorted my things.

PIERRE:
I chucked them.

MATHILDE:
You threw out some of my things?

PIERRE:
Those that could hurt you.

MATHILDE:
What right did you have?

PIERRE:
An oncologist's right.

MATHILDE:
I'm leaving. Lena will have cigarettes.

PIERRE:
You're going to Lena's?

MATHILDE:
What's it to you?

PIERRE:
Will you tell her what you just told me?

MATHILDE:
What?

PIERRE:
That you won't write.

MATHILDE:
Maybe.

PIERRE:
She'll despise you.

MATHILDE:
Of course not...

PIERRE:
If you're not writing, you're no good to her.

MATHILDE:
She's not just my publisher. She's my friend.

PIERRE:
Don't tell me you believe that! The boss is never the employee's friend.

MATHILDE:
We're talking about art not a factory.

PIERRE:
Go ahead! Race over there and tell her that Mathilde Esnault won't be writing the follow-up to her scandalous life, go ahead! I'd be surprised if she offered you any cigarettes. Why do you think so many artists signed that petition? They're interested in your story, they want to know more, Lena's promised it to them, and now she's waiting for you to prove you're up to it...

MATHILDE:
Lena respects me. That's why she came on visiting day.

PIERRE:
You amaze me! The number of dinner parties your incarceration rescued from tedium!

MATHILDE:
How would you know?

PIERRE:
I was on the outside.

MATHILDE:
People were talking about me?

PIERRE:

At intermission at the theatre, over cocktails at book-signings, in the writers' association cafeteria, oh, you have no idea what's in store for you!

MATHILDE:

Lena came every visiting day, for three months.

PIERRE:

One has to feed the rumour mill. Did she wear her houndstooth suit or something sporty?

MATHILDE:

She looked elegant. To please and honour me. She respects me.

PIERRE:

Not you. What you write. But I love you… when you insult your computer, when you bite your nails, when you wake up in the morning and you still have sheet marks on your cheeks–

MATHILDE: (interrupting)

And you laugh at me. Your favourite after-dinner joke was: "I cure the dying. My wife – Mathilde – kills off characters."

PIERRE:

I was still there to comfort you.

MATHILDE:

Comfort me? From what?

PIERRE:

Your nightmares, your setbacks, your obsessions…

MATHILDE:

I've always thought you'd love it if I had a nervous breakdown.

PIERRE:

When you had nightmares I held your hand, I brought you a drink and you said: "If we'd had children, you'd have devoted less time to me."

MATHILDE:

I'm sure I felt like a child, not a wife.

PIERRE:

You were a wife, for thirteen years!

MATHILDE:

Yes, a doctor's wife! I'm going. Lena will be worried.

PIERRE:

Tell me! When will you dare tell her?

MATHILDE:

I think she already suspects.

PIERRE:

Did you say it? In the visiting room?

MATHILDE:

In the visiting room, she gave me news from outside, she opened a window for me and I breathed. I didn't see her to talk about my cell!

PIERRE:

She brought you oxygen like you were a coma patient.

MATHILDE:

Think what you like! I'm going.

PIERRE:

She kept you on life support, so you'd still be useful.

MATHILDE: *(ironic)*
That's it!

PIERRE:
You're in for a shock.

MATHILDE:
When?

PIERRE:
When you've lost Lena's respect. She's going to wait for you to write. Each day she'll get a bit more disappointed, after a while she'll let you know she needs to be alone again, then she'll politely show you the door, the way you'd deal with an old lover… it's pathetic.

MATHILDE:
And you? What are you offering me? Boxes? A house that doesn't exist. Chinese food?

PIERRE:
If you stay here you'll rediscover your routine, your world and your novelist's reflexes - the coffee I make you in the morning before I go to the hospital, your desk facing the wall, your trinkets, your thick socks, your sweaters, the phone calls you need to make when you take a break, your spontaneous ten-minute naps, and our evenings out when you reinvented yourself so you could wake up the next day, ready to write. At Lena's? She'll have set everything up without knowing your habits, she'll keep an eye on you, and you'll feel her gaze, weighing on you like you're in prison.

A beat.

MATHILDE:
What time is it?

PIERRE:

One in the morning. Do you think you can show up there at one in the morning?

MATHILDE:

I don't know. I didn't think it was so late.

PIERRE:

You're going to show up there at one in the morning already making excuses… "Sorry… I'm bothering you…" She'll say no, already regretting her invitation, the strain will begin, and the admiration will end.

MATHILDE:

What if I called?

PIERRE:

Calling in the middle of the night? That's worse. (*He stands, goes to a cupboard, takes a pack of cigarettes, offers it to her.*) Here! I just remembered this pack… (*she lights a cigarette*) We'll put a bed in your office. I won't go in. Are you sleepy?

MATHILDE:

I'm exhausted.

PIERRE:

You can sleep here, no strings attached. You can take off tomorrow without telling me.

MATHILDE:

I've gotten used to waking up early. I sleep for shorter and shorter periods.

A beat. Pierre watches her smoke.

PIERRE:

Yes… everything can be… that familiar again… This is your home.

MATHILDE:

Yes…

PIERRE:

You act like you've forgotten. Your home. You can wake up, put on a CD, reheat some pasta, take a shower…

MATHILDE:

I've forgotten how to do so many things.

PIERRE:

I'm used to that – when you weren't writing, you barely noticed what you were doing. (*MATHILDE smiles.*) Remember the day you dropped your purse down the garbage chute?

MATHILDE:

Yes!

PIERRE:

Or the night you went out without your shoes on?

MATHILDE:

I knew something was wrong, but I couldn't figure out what… I thought: "Something's not right – but what is it?"

PIERRE:

What I loved was when you said: "Work went well." I'd pour you a glass of wine, you'd light a cigarette and… and that's it. Hardly anything.

MATHILDE:

When work went well… everything about the day seemed right.

PIERRE:

Yes, it was right... harmonious, like hitting the right note...

MATHILDE:

There's no evening in prison. At six-thirty they serve dinner. Then it's over. There's no transition between day and night... Everything's so brutal, with no subtlety... I thought often of our glass of wine...

PIERRE:

Do you want one...? Do you want me to pour you one?

MATHILDE:

No.

PIERRE:

Listen, we should get drunk, get good and plastered!

MATHILDE:

You're a sad drunk.

PIERRE:

Yes, but you're a happy drunk. When you drink you say the stupidest things. I love it when you lose control... don't you think it would be better if we stopped controlling things?

MATHILDE:

Stop playing games, I'm tired, I'm not in the mood.

PIERRE:

I'm not playing games... I dream of seeing us let go.

A beat.

PIERRE:
There's one question no one asked you... and that I couldn't bring myself to.

MATHILDE:
Yes...?

PIERRE:
Did you... with him... I know what happened, at the hotel... what I mean – goddammit! (*a beat.*) Did you sleep with him?

MATHILDE:
Sleep?

PIERRE:
You went to bed together, but did you sleep together? I mean, for long? For hours? The night?

MATHILDE:
For hours? No. Why are you smiling?

PIERRE:
Because if he didn't sleep with you, he doesn't know.

MATHILDE:
What?

PIERRE:
He doesn't know... (*a beat*) You'll get in touch with Lena. I'll make sure you get in touch.

MATHILDE:
As of tomorrow.

PIERRE:
No, definitely not tomorrow, it would spoil everything.

MATHILDE:
Why?

PIERRE:
Because you don't realize.

MATHILDE:
What?

PIERRE:
Your state.

MATHILDE:
You don't think I'm up to it?

PIERRE:
No. You're at the beginning of recovery. You remind me of some
of my patients.

MATHILDE:
Cancer patients?

PIERRE:
They're like you. They drift around in their bodies, with that
faraway look. And they're cold too. No, you should get in touch
with her, but with your head held high. Do you remember?
When we'd go on vacation?

MATHILDE:
What?

PIERRE:
The calls you'd get from Lena? "So? How's it going? Will you
have something to give me when you get back?" Or better still:
"Denis Vaillant handed in his latest novel. It's a masterpiece. Did

you know Julia's working on something new?" So, you'd start spinning like a moth in the dark. Everything made you anxious - the sun, the beach, the noisy tourists...

MATHILDE:
I remember.

PIERRE:
You stopped enjoying everything and in the end... we'd have to come home.

MATHILDE:
That's true.

PIERRE:
How many times have you told me you'd die if you stopped writing?

MATHILDE:
Maybe that's because I've never started living – you just said so, even on vacation...

PIERRE:
An affair... three months in a refrigerator... more than ninety nights of fear... and nothing to write about?

He picks up a pen and notepad.

MATHILDE:
I'm not going to write a how-to book for jailed VIPs or the true story of "the scandal that wrecked my career"! It's ridiculous!

PIERRE:
Why not simply admit your fear?

MATHILDE:
What are you writing?

PIERRE:
I'll read it to you after.

MATHILDE:
Are you observing me?

PIERRE:
Don't be paranoid.

MATHILDE:
Are you going to tell the papers what happened here tonight?

PIERRE:
Have I talked to the papers?

MATHILDE:
You said: "I'll be strong."

PIERRE:
And wasn't I?

MATHILDE:
You didn't come to see me.

PIERRE:
So that you wouldn't be humiliated. The visiting room. The strip search. The rules.

MATHILDE:
A presence. A glance. A sign you're still part of the world of the living. Your so-called strength was a repudiation.

PIERRE: *(notes this)*
Yes. Of what?

MATHILDE:
I won't answer you if you're writing.

He puts down the pen.

PIERRE:
There.

MATHILDE:
Your strength was a eunuch's strength, Pontius Pilate with clean hands.

PIERRE:
You missed me.

MATHILDE:
No.

PIERRE:
You waited for me, and as soon as you got out this is where you came.

MATHILDE:
To pick up my things.

PIERRE:
You could have sent Lena.

MATHILDE:
I didn't know which way to go... I went to the first place that came to mind, the most familiar.

PIERRE:

Your home. *(he picks up the pen.)* Maybe you don't need to write to dwell on things, but to redeem yourself.

MATHILDE:

But I'm not ashamed.

PIERRE:

He is.

MATHILDE:

Who's "he"?

PIERRE:

Your student. At the trial he said he was sorry. That you seduced him.

MATHILDE:

That's not true.

PIERRE:

He said he was ashamed to have been seduced.

MATHILDE:

That's not true. I didn't hear him say that.

PIERRE:

Oh... Then I read it in the paper. It's true that he wasn't in great shape the day of the trial... not very talkative... He looked fifteen.

MATHILDE:

Neither of us was ever ashamed. We were swept away, together. His parents generated that shame, not him. Never. What are you doing? Are you taking notes on what I'm saying?

PIERRE:
Don't worry about it.

MATHILDE:
What are you going to do with those notes?

PIERRE:
Sell them to Lena! *(he laughs)* Silly goose! Jacques – we'll call him "Jacques" – said that you were always available.

MATHILDE:
Always.

PIERRE:
That you reserved and paid for the hotel.

MATHILDE:
Obviously.

PIERRE:
Were you aware of the seriousness of the situation?

MATHILDE:
I was aware of how dull my life had become, as though instead of living, I was copying other people, waiting for old age to rear its head.

PIERRE:
What did you do together?

MATHILDE: *(ironic)*
Some tidying.

PIERRE:
Did you fuck?

MATHILDE:
That word doesn't suit you. You have to say it with joy and appetite.

PIERRE:
I'll work at it. How did you fuck?

MATHILDE:
Like I'd never dared.

PIERRE:
Dared what?

MATHILDE:
I dared not to be decent. Beautiful. I dared to make faces. To laugh. To talk. To smoke. To be had from behind.

PIERRE:
From behind?

MATHILDE:
I wasn't afraid of him being behind me. Of him seeing everything I couldn't. The nape of my neck. My ass. Pimples, maybe. A stretch mark. My body…

A beat.

PIERRE:
Your body?

MATHILDE:
It was an offering. There to be taken.

PIERRE:
Be more precise.

MATHILDE:

I felt my shape as though I was touching it myself, and just being there... that's right... THERE, lying on the bed, was already a pleasure. I was in my body and outside it... I was with him but... with myself as well, like never, like I... Like I was meeting myself.

PIERRE:

And then?

MATHILDE:

I felt full, voluptuous *(she laughs)* even though I wasn't... My body was able to go where I wanted it to, without resisting, it anticipated, it invented–

PIERRE:

Positions?

MATHILDE:

A way of being. Always beautiful.

PIERRE:

What did you like the most?

MATHILDE:

When he lay on top of me. When he shoved inside me. Hard. When everything shifted... With him, everything shifted, everything opened up...

PIERRE:

I don't understand.

MATHILDE:

We were able to spark something outside of time, that had no relation to real life, because... the meaning was different.

PIERRE:
What meaning? The meaning of what?

MATHILDE:
The meaning of time and of action, mostly.

PIERRE:
Yes, actions. But surely that's irrational. Were you
becoming irrational?

MATHILDE:
No. Just someone else – or, rather myself. I became another me.

PIERRE:
A schizophrenic split.

MATHILDE:
Oh! Less so than writing.

PIERRE:
Really? How was it different than writing?

MATHILDE:
It was less structured than writing. And more shameless.

PIERRE:
Writing is shameless.

MATHILDE:
But masked.

PIERRE:
You were masked with him as well. Your life with me, with your
novels, those lives were masked.

MATHILDE:
They melted away.

PIERRE:
Nonetheless they were part of you.

MATHILDE:
It no longer mattered.

PIERRE:
But they were there. In the part of you that said it was time to
come home, that remembered to return the room key.

MATHILDE:
Once that key was returned, I didn't give a damn what was waiting.

PIERRE:
You didn't give a damn because it was taken for granted. I was
taken for granted. And I was your reality.

MATHILDE:
I didn't need you.

PIERRE:
Yes! More than ever! You told me so, you told me I was your
anchor, something safe, something stable.

MATHILDE:
I said that because I lacked confidence, because I thought writing
wasn't important, that I liked it so much it couldn't be work. I
needed a solid counterbalance, I guess…

PIERRE:
Let's get back to your relationship with Jacques.

MATHILDE:

I'm tired, I've had enough.

PIERRE:

So it was unstructured and shameless.

MATHILDE:

Leave me alone.

PIERRE:

Do you miss it? (*a beat*) I'm asking you if you miss it.

MATHILDE:

Yes!

PIERRE:

Did you realize how much power you had over him?

MATHILDE:

I'm telling you that's enough!

PIERRE:

Did you hold yourself accountable?

MATHILDE:

For that experience? Yes! Completely accountable!

PIERRE:

No, for your power... for your influence! Do you have any idea
what you led that boy into? Didn't you realize how serious it was?

MATHILDE:

Now you're talking like his parents!

PIERRE:
You went to the trial in the same frame of mind as when you forgot your shoes: "Something's wrong, but what?" Are you listening?

MATHILDE:
No.

PIERRE:
No? And why not? Why not? What are you thinking of?

MATHILDE:
A word... that we'd made up, in need of something of our own – we had no place, no past, no future, so we made up a word.

PIERRE:
What was the word?

She smiles. A pause.

PIERRE:
Well... At any rate, there was a scandal.

MATHILDE:
That won't stop me from doing it again.

PIERRE:
You're insane! It would be...! It would be a humiliation!

MATHILDE:
For whom?

PIERRE:
Well... for you, of course! Are you ready to humiliate yourself, again?

MATHILDE:
Oh my God, yes!

PIERRE:
For how long?

MATHILDE:
Long enough to see him again.

A pause. MATHILDE holds her head in her hands.

PIERRE:
Are you tired?

MATHILDE:
It's been quite a day… it's stupid to say, but… it's not easy to leave that place… the rift that occurs – it's inexplicably lonely.

PIERRE:
Of course. Of course. Shall I make a bed up in the office?

MATHILDE:
Please.

PIERRE:
Shall I run you a bath?

MATHILDE:
A bath? No…

PIERRE:
Did you take something to help you sleep… In that place?

MATHILDE:
Oh yes.

PIERRE:
I'll leave a sleeping pill on the desk.

MATHILDE:
Thank you.

He gets up. Places the notebook in front of MATHILDE and leaves. A pause. She lights a cigarette, then notices the notebook. Reads it. Pierre returns.

PIERRE:
I left you two blankets and... did you read it?

MATHILDE:
I read it.

PIERRE:
It's interesting, isn't it? What do you think?

MATHILDE:
I disagree.

PIERRE:
You and I spoke... freely, didn't we?

MATHILDE:
I disagree. I didn't say that.

PIERRE:
Nonetheless it's what I took down.

MATHILDE points to the notebook.

MATHILDE:

Those sentences aren't mine. I didn't speak in the present tense. I didn't say: "I feel my shape as though I'm touching it myself"... or: "I'm shameless."

PIERRE:

We'll re-read it tomorrow.

MATHILDE:

"I want to be humiliated!" I never said that!

PIERRE:

Of course... you must be right...

MATHILDE:

It all comes off so cold... so calculated...

PIERRE:

I'm sorry, I was mistaken. You're going to write about what you really experienced... in that place, and with Jacques.

MATHILDE:

Why?

PIERRE:

Because... It's like the dates you wrote down in your day book... those long stretches of time, that were yours alone – isn't that what you said? Write about what you experienced... it's a bit like experiencing it again – but free.

MATHILDE:

But why would you want me to write about it?

PIERRE:

So that you won't need it any more. (*a pause*) Mathilde, you
know... I didn't tidy your things so you could take them away. I
did it to be with them. To touch them. Understand them.

MATHILDE:

Oh, Pierre! It would have been better for you to work, find
new patients.

PIERRE:

I don't know if my patients left me or if I left them... I don't
know if your parents called or if I imagined it... and most of all I
don't know why I didn't go inside that prison... I went, often, I'd
stand outside for hours, for no reason, so the time would
swallow me up. (*a pause*) But the one thing I do know, is that
without you... I have no meaning. Stay. This is where you need
to be. Like before.

MATHILDE:

But I'm different...

PIERRE:

You'll write about it.

MATHILDE:

I'm tired... disappointed...

PIERRE:

You'll write about it. Come with me. (*a beat*) Come and sleep.

MATHILDE:

Tell me the truth, Pierre.

PIERRE:

Yes?

MATHILDE:
Is this... love...?

PIERRE:
Let's go.

MATHILDE:
Is it?

PIERRE:
Shh...

Pierre takes Mathilde's arm and leads her from the room which remains dark.

THE END

About the playwright:

Véronique Olmi has been writing for the theatre for over ten years. She is the author of ten plays for stage and radio, many of which have been translated into several languages. Her work has been staged by some of France's most distinguished directors. In 1998, *Chaos debout* enjoyed particular acclaim in the production directed by Jacques Lassalle at the Avignon Festival. Notable productions of *Point à la ligne* and *Le Passage* were followed most recently by Gildas Bourdet's production of *Le Jardin des apparences* which earned a nomination for the prestigious Molière Prize (category Best Playwright) in 2002. Véronique Olmi is also the author of a collection of short stories (1998) and three novels published in France by les Éditions Actes Sud.

About the translator:

Morwyn Brebner's plays include *Music for Contortionist* (co-produced by the Shaw Festival and the Tarragon Theatre in 2000); the book and lyrics for the musical *Little Mercy's First Murder* (seven Dora Mavor Moore awards); and *The Optimists,* first produced at Theatre Junction in Calgary (nominated for five Betty Mitchell awards) and subsequently produced at Tarragon Theatre in September 2005. Other translations include *Strawberries in January* by Evelyne de la Chenelière. She recently co-wrote, with Ken Finkleman and Ellen Vanstone, a six-part miniseries for CBC television. She is a graduate of the National Theatre School of Canada and a playwright-in-residence at Tarragon Theatre in Toronto. Her newest play is *The Pessimist.*

THE LIGHTHOUSE

(Le Phare)

By Timothée de Fombelle

Translated by Don Hannah
Based on a line translation by Glen Nichols

Production Information:

Le Phare was first produced at the Théâtre du Marais in Paris in September 2001. It was directed by Nicole Aubry and featured Clément Sibony.

The Lighthouse, the English-language version of **Le Phare**, was workshopped and read at the Banff playRites Colony in May 2004. It was read by Kevin MacDonald. Linda Gaboriau acted as translation dramatruge.

In February 2005, **The Lighthouse** was invited to be part of the National Arts Centre's (Ottawa) International Reading Series. Don Hannah directed the reading; Jeff Lawson read.

He is alone.

In the winter, at six, we light up the big room. Up top stays lit day and night.

In the winter, we never let the lantern up there go out, but the big room lamps get put out for a few hours just to say it's the day. And at six, we light three lamps, it's nighttime. With my brother here, there were four. Now my father says three's enough.

When I'm sick, they're lit in the day. That's happened a hundred times, the lamp shining there by my bedside in the daytime, at two. The flame's so small, but it warms up the whole room, and my blankets, and my hands. It's the light that warms me up. My father says that, too - the light warms up the downstairs, not the heat. We never see heat here. In the summer, the downstairs is a cellar with thick walls, and the heat stays outside with the wind.

In the summer, nothing gets lit till ten - the big lantern, too. In the winter, at six, we light up the big room. Up top stays lit day and night. Nobody knows the darkness here on the ocean in winter. At night, the grey just falls darker, and the clouds push down, coal black.

One time my brother read this book that said the sea and the sky can get mixed together, then the horizon isn't there any more. But that's wrong. I stay because the horizon stays. The sea and the sky are never the same. My brother believed that book, but they're both wrong. The sea's pointy, and sharp as rocks. The sky curves all above it. You can't mix them up.

Where the points jab at the curve, that place, that's the horizon. That's why I'm here. When I can't see the horizon anymore, if it gets swollen like the sky or scratchy like the sea, when there's no horizon left, then I go to sleep so I can find it, so I won't do like my brother. I leave the grey and the wind so I won't lose the horizon. That's when I get sick, and I light the lamp in daytime.

On those days, my father stays round the lighthouse. On other days, he checks his snares at the far side of the island, in the thorn bushes, one hour in the morning and one hour in the evening. He snares rabbits.

The rabbits are alone on the island with the birds and us. The dog died in December.

Before my father came, there were no rabbits. He brought three with him, two girls and a boy. Now, they're everywhere, a hundred of them, and us, and the birds. The only ones that leave, birds, they come and go. They sit there on the cliffs, or they fly, their feathers and droppings all over the rocks, white like sea foam.

The dog died in December. He died out in the rain. Of nothing, my father said, he died of nothing. Not old or sick, he just died, period. Dead. On the days when I lose the horizon, I'm afraid I could die of nothing.

On Wednesday, the man from the Coast Guard comes with the crates. He drags his boat up on the beach in the cove, on the pebbles. He used to give me little sugars wrapped in paper when I was small. In December, my father told him I was big. Now I only have ordinary sugar, like for morning coffee, or in the afternoon, maybe.

There are four crates: three with groceries like potatoes, beets, swiss chard, corn, some other vegetables, and coffee - things like that. The other one has supplies for the lighthouse and for us: clothes, maybe, and soap, matches - like that. The crates, every Wednesday at ten - it's the best.

The man from the Coast Guard used to bring books for my brother. Then he would take them away the next Wednesday. So, Thursday, everything got read; Saturday, everything got read again. And my brother waiting for the crates; waiting for books, and me for my little sugars. And now, nothing. But crates are still crates, and Wednesday is different - it's the best.

I have eyes that won't read. I know my letters, I learned them, I know A and B and all the others, WXYZ, but my eyes won't read. I lose the letters inside the words, and the words inside the lines, and then the lines get lost in the page. When I find the word again, I stop and get lost in the picture it makes.

My brother used to tell me not to think too much about the pictures in the words, just look at each word fast then go to the next. But I can't just go from one to the next because I have eyes that won't read. So those books from the man from the Coast Guard - they mean nothing to me. I still have this ripped out page with lots of words on it. There's "gentle" and "shelf" and "pumpkin." There's "pebble" and fifty others. There's "honest." I don't let them run together, I look at each one all by itself. Honest.

My father doesn't read. It's not his eyes, it's him. He never learned the ABCs, he doesn't know. Honest.

My brother told me that if I didn't think too much about the picture in each word, if I just let them all go by, then I would get one big picture that moves, like it's real. He said that there could even be a smell, like soup maybe. And that there could even be a taste like soup, like it's real. But I already have the smell and the taste and all that in one word alone. Honest.

Now, it's the winter. At six, we light up the big room. Up top stays lit day and night. It turns, up there, the lantern lights up the whole sea. Not a scrap shines downstairs. The whole sea, and nothing in the big room.

When my father leaves me to check his snares - that hour in the morning, and again in the evening - he tells me that I'm in charge, that I'm an employee of lighthouses and buoys. He says this is why he shares the crates with me.

While my father checks his snares at the far side of the island, I go up by the big lantern and keep watch. I tell myself that this is why I get my share of the crates.

Before, my brother used to work mornings and I took evenings, or we were on guard together. Now, there's just me doing both. Some nights, my father and I can't eat all the rabbit. We used to give some to the dog, but the dog died of nothing in December. So now we throw the leftover rabbit into the sea.

My brother left in the summer. He got the idea looking out at the horizon; he said if he was there, where it was, he would never let it go.

When I got sick, he told stories about mountains and towns. He said he would go there. He got the idea a long time ago. I never got the idea.

My brother left the last summer. The last summer the wind stayed on the island, and so strong that the sun was cold, and the whole summer was gone before we could even see it.

The other summers, for a little bit, sun with no clouds and the wind went away, and the ocean lay still. And red flowers on the thorns. We were outdoors, all day long, those other summers. Everyone went to check the snares, all three of us, with only the dog left behind at the lighthouse, by himself. When we came back, he'd get two live rabbits to chase. He'd try to stuff them both inside his little yap. He'd finish off one, greedy, but the other was already watching under the rocks. My father was in a summer mood, too, smiling some days, and even talking more. Those summers my brother read only at night and outdoors. We went to hide in the hole in the cliff; threw stones down in the cove, made the rabbits swim. I slept all night without waking up and ran back outside every morning. I even forgot about the crates coming, and Wednesdays I was surprised by the man from the Coast Guard. I forgot about the sugars in my pocket with the ants, and I forgot to look at the horizon, and my brother forgot his books, and his mountains and his towns.

The rabbits swim, only their ears stick out. The dog never learned how to swim. He waits on shore while the rabbit swims around and round to keep from getting eaten. The dog never moves. The rabbit sinks, his ears go down below the water; he'd rather do that than end up in the greedy yap. My father didn't like the rabbits in the water. We did it anyway, just to see how long they could go.

This one time, a rabbit turned his back on the dog and us, and the shore. He was swimming so calm, he swam straight out to sea, a hundred yards and we could still see him. Then we lost sight of him. He's still out there, I bet, still swimming straight ahead. Honest.

But none of that last summer. The sun never touched the island. My brother stayed in his books everyday. Wednesday, the man from the Coast Guard; Thursday, everything got read; Saturday, read again; and, all the other days, nothing but waiting. I ate my little sugars, all at once, right there on the shore, and spent the rest of the week waiting.

Last summer the wind never went away. No summer for us at all. My father never said a word, I was sick all the time, and my brother annoying and waiting.

The summer was gone before we had time to see it. And that's when my brother left, on Wednesday.

I was out checking the snares with my father. My brother was in charge, the employee of lighthouses and buoys along with the dog. I didn't forget about the crates and the little sugars, but I thought the man from the Coast Guard would come later, after the snares. I didn't say good bye to my brother.

When we looked in the bushes, all empty snares, no rabbits. My father said that, "No rabbits."

We moved the snares around to other bushes farther away, it took a long time. When we were going back, we saw the black spot of the man from the Coast Guard's boat way out at sea. "He's coming," I said.

"Leaving," said my father.

And he was.

I stared at the Coast Guard boat, and I thought about the crates. I ran back across the island. My father was walking way behind me. Rabbits were running all over the place. I was thinking about the sugars in their paper. All across the island, the wind kept slowing me down.

The lighthouse was getting bigger, and the black spot of the Coast Guard boat smaller out at sea. I looked at my brother up in the lantern room without seeing him there. I opened the downstairs door without seeing him inside, just the crates, all four, with groceries and supplies, and my little sugars wrapped in newspaper, but no books. I ate half my sugars, and stuck the rest in my pocket with the ants. When there's wind, my brother stays inside and reads, but no one's downstairs. I ran up the stairs, round and round, all the way to the top. No one.

From up top, I could see the whole island. I saw the dog down on the cove looking out to sea, like before with the swimming rabbits. I ran down the staircase, round and down. My father was putting the groceries in the cupboard, and the supplies in the wooden chest. I didn't say a word, I ran down to the cove. I watched the sea with the dog, like before with the swimming rabbits.

The black mark of the boat was all gone from the horizon. Then the horizon was all gone. The sky and the sea were all the same. Then I got sick.

When I woke up, there was the downstairs, but with three lamps not four. It was six at night, broad daylight still, but windy grey. My father didn't come back till nine. He told me my brother wasn't on the island anymore. He'd been calling him for eleven hours and looking everywhere. He told me that he must have fallen off the cliff and, with all this wind, he would've drowned.

I thought about the rabbits, not the ones that sank, but the one who swam away. My brother never used to fall off the cliff, and he never used to drown. My father said that he would wait until the next Wednesday to ask the man from the Coast Guard to tell the authorities, and to put a cross on the cliff. I stopped listening. I was thinking about the little sugars in my pocket and I ate them all.

My father cooked some vegetables without any rabbit. I finished all my supper; I was almost asleep when I heard something smash. My father said, "Go back to sleep, it's nothing."

But I know what I heard; he broke a plate, and something was stuck inside his throat, like crying.

That was Wednesday, and I was sick till Sunday. Couldn't get up or even go out before that. Then Sunday evening, I looked out the downstairs window for the first time. I thought I heard the wind stop blowing a draft under the door, but it must've only turned around because the sea was white and pointy. Two days and three nights before Wednesday, before the authorities will be told to take my brother off their lists, before maybe a cross on the cliff. I kept thinking about it. Honest. And the little sugars, and to see if there were crates with books, I wanted to see.

Monday, my father reset the snares. This time, too many rabbits. He gave some to the dog, but the dog only left the cove at nighttime now. He didn't chase the rabbits, it wasn't in him. They ran all over the beach, free as the breeze.

On Wednesday, at four in the morning I was waiting already. At ten, way out, there was a black spot. It was getting closer, growing bigger, a grey shape first, then the boat. It scraped the pebbles. The man from the Coast Guard beached it a few feet; he carried the crates, one by one, and put them on shore. There was a little package wrapped in newspaper, and no books. I wouldn't take anything, I didn't touch a thing. My father was checking his snares. I watched the man from the Coast Guard. He smiled and pointed to the little sugars in newspaper. I still didn't touch a thing.

I asked him finally if my brother had gone back with him in the boat last Wednesday. He gave me a big smile and said, "Your brother?" Then he laughed and said, "When did you get a brother?"

I asked again without really paying attention. He was grinning and saying, "I'd know after all these Wednesdays, if you had a brother."

I asked him again. And he laughed and laughed, then he left, and the boat got smaller, the black spot disappeared again.

Then I hid in the hole in the cliff. I could hear my father calling me. I didn't answer him till noon. He thought I'd gone away, too. I would have liked to, but I never got the idea.

I didn't come out till noon. My father was happy to find me, with enough words to make me believe him. He told me he talked to the man from the Coast Guard, and that my brother was dead for sure, that he was the body they found on the beach on the mainland.

I never cried before, and I didn't then because there was no way my father could have spoken to the man from the Coast Guard: I never took my eyes off that man from the time his boat first appeared on the horizon till it disappeared after he left. It was a lie, his death, my brother's. That cliff never let anyone fall.

But that didn't stop my father from making a cross out of an oar, worm holes and rotten with salt, and sticking it on the cliff. I saw it from up in the lantern room. I saw that cross nailed together with a piece of string and my father standing beside it.

I didn't say anything sad during supper or afterwards ever.

The fall might've come, but the seasons on the island are nothing but a calendar, except for winter and summer sometimes, and some years everything's all the same, only one season, wind and rain, one after the other, or both at the same time, or a storm where you can't tell the wind from the rain, or the rain from the wind, when the light can't get past the railing up at the top of the lighthouse, and we live like rabbits without any rabbits to eat, and the crates can't get here until the next Tuesday or Wednesday, so we eat the emergency cans from the back cupboard like they're something special, waiting for the wind to separate from the rain or the other way round, waiting for the sea to lie flat.

The fall came and went, all grey with rain and wind but no big storm.

I never spoke, not anymore. Just to the dog, to tell him that this looking out at the sea is no way to live, that they would come back, the rabbit and my brother, they'd just gone to see the mountains and the towns like he said, and they would come back after. Then the dog would be given rabbits to chase, and my brother would read and tell stories about the mountains and towns again, and maybe about windmills and girls.

Windmills, I knew about them because of what my brother told me from the books, about what gets put inside them, and then how bread comes out, bread with insides soft like a sponge. I stopped being mad at the wind for blowing cause I thought of the wheels it was turning to make bread. I imagined them from the books. But girls, I'd even seen one.

The girl who came sometimes with the man from the Coast Guard, his friend, not all that much older than me. At first, she was hiding, like a periwinkle all curled up in a black shell. You think, this Wednesday is like any other, just the same. You see the black spot, then the man from the Coast Guard in his boat, then the crates and the little newspaper sugars, but then, when you look closer at the boat now so close to the shore - what's that, sitting there near the back with a red cloth and those eyes below it? Sitting there, all curled up inside that oilskin, the one that belongs to the man. And there, coming out from inside that dark oilskin, those two hands rubbing together, and eyes that are looking at me like a rabbit from under the rocks, but maybe smiling.

The first time, my father, who never talks said, "Who's the girl?"

And I heard everything, it was a girl, and I'd never seen one. And there I was, seeing one.

On another Wednesday, the man brought us sweaters. It was the girl who made them, his friend who came sometimes, always curled up near the back of the boat. I said thank you, and then I wore that sweater every day, thinking about those two hands that were making it.

Since the end of summer, there's been no one else on the boat, just the man from the Coast Guard alone at the front. I didn't mean to, really, but after my brother left, I connected that with him. I couldn't think about my brother in the town or the mountain without seeing the red cloth and those eyes right there beside him.

The weather was getting colder and colder. Because the summer was gone before we saw it, nothing warmed up the sea, and going outside meant cracked skin and noses like cold little pebbles. The snares were empty with rabbits, and my father only checked them twice a week. He stayed inside the lighthouse, older than before, and I went out every day, just the same, down to the cove with the dog to wait.

Wednesdays came later than ever. Time was so slow now. Even the time between two waves coming in was as long as it used to take for six. Time was so long and slow. Wednesdays were more special than ever. When I ate one of my sugars, I'd look at the three others, and make myself wait: a hundred waves before I could eat the second, then two hundred before the next, like that, but a hundred waves seemed like a thousand, and the sugar taste in my mouth went away so fast. I looked all around, counted the waves, looked at all the pebbles on the beach. They never got bored. I envied them so much, and the dog, too, and the sea, rolling on and on its whole life.

I got the idea of going away. But what about my brother? He might come back with stories of mountains and towns, windmills, and with the girl, maybe.

The girl. I would recognize her from far away on the beach. I would pick the thorns off my sweater and not know what to look like in front of her because she's standing up now. She's watching me walk towards them. She's pulled her hands inside her sleeves. And my brother is grinning, and poking at a pebble with his toe.

I thought they would come back, the both of them, and the girl would take off the red cloth when she came inside the downstairs for a visit.

Even with the cloth in her hand, I would still know her girl eyes and mouth, closer together than others, with her white face and the red still glowing there.

Someone tells her, "This is everything, this room, and the stairs, and the lantern room up top."

Then we climb round and round and when we go outside, she puts the red cloth on crooked, up there in the wind. I show her the whole island, the hole in the cliff, the far side with the thorns. The dog would be doing his chasing, and she would say that's mean, just like my father, but she would laugh all the same at the silly rabbit under the rocks.

I made all that up to make the waiting easier, but it didn't, and the waves didn't come any faster between the little sugars, and for the first time I was bored. I didn't understand how I could be missing those books. I have eyes that won't read.

Winter came so slow with too much time to see it.

Everything else is in December and I'm here one more hour.

Everything happened this month, in one day mostly, except for the dog three days before. I left him down on the beach in the cove because the rain was so hard it was like needles, it went through my underwear, soaking my hide. The dog was wetter than me, and I called him twice to come inside, but he stayed down there watching the sea that you couldn't even see anymore, stayed down there under the storm, all silent.

I sat down in the armchair with my back to the window. My father made Sunday dinner, with vegetables but no rabbit, like the time before at the end of summer after my brother left. My father who never talks, except serious, said this thing like never before, like he's singing, "The crates on Wednesday, come for the holiday!"

And I was thinking that the last two Wednesdays, there were no little sugars because I'm too big now. But I was in my chair counting, and he was right, Wednesday was twenty-four on the calendar, the holiday crates would have more groceries - chicken and those cans of candy fruit, that are terrible really, but special. They come from the senior citizens club but I'm not sure what that is. I was thinking about that, about the senior citizens club, about Christmas the day after, and I thought what was that, too.

My father sat down for supper and then I said I was going to look for the dog. He was dead. And when I came back that's when my father said you could die of nothing.

I ate my supper, and I thought about the island staying here for the birds, for the rabbits and us. I saw myself not falling sick or anything, I thought about my dream of wanting to be a pebble, and

I believed I was one. Monday and Tuesday weren't all that long,
almost short, almost nothing. Pebbles can wait - pebble is a virtue.

Time stopped and was hard now, like the pebbles' time. No
Wednesdays, or holiday crates from the senior citizens' club. Just
pictures of the dog, my brother's stories, and the eyes of the red cloth.

Wednesday was the day when I really saw that everything was
leaving like the end of a story.

I saw from far away that two men were on the black spot of the
boat, the man from the Coast Guard and another. The new one had
a coat that wasn't oilskin, more like blankets, and his hat was
slipping down. He had this smile while he looked all around the
island, as if it were somewhere special or dirty. He nearly lost his
balance on the boat and was holding onto a box.

He called the man from the Coast Guard, "Coast Guard," like
that was his name.

"Thank you Coast Guard. Thank you very much Coast Guard;
Coast Guard please wait for me. It's not that I don't like this place
but I don't know how to swim."

Then he laughed like a bunch of birds. And the man from the
Coast Guard unloaded five packed holiday crates.

My father came out of the lighthouse and watched the new man,
squeezing his eyes tight like he was trying to see far away or look at
the sun. I followed that man. He shook my father's hand. He said he
was the representative of lighthouses and buoys and that he'd come
with something important. My father told me to take the holiday
crates up to the downstairs. I took them, one after the other,
without even looking inside. I watched my father listen to the
representative, and my father in his sweater was looking out at the
horizon and his head was saying no.

The man was showing some papers that he kept holding against
his coat so they wouldn't blow away. My father was standing
straight and tall. The man from the Coast Guard joined them; and
me, too. The representative was telling my father he didn't have a
choice; he kept pushing his hat down in the wind. The man from
the Coast Guard said he would come and get us next Wednesday,

that it was good it was finally over, all the Wednesday crossings, especially now his wife was having a baby on New Year's. I saw the red cloth in my mind.

My father stopped saying no with his head, he just kept looking at the horizon, then he went back into the downstairs and the man said, "Till Wednesday."

And they left. I heard the representative getting into the boat saying, "Hey, Coast Guard, be careful, I can't swim!" and he laughed again like screechy birds.

When I went inside, my father was putting away the crates, and I could feel something like the end of a story. The day went by. My father never said a word. And not the same silence like before, it was heavy, more scary, with more wanting to talk but not knowing how. At supper my father was looking more at my plate than his own, wanting to announce something big. There were silences, where he was staring at a forkful of senior citizens chicken halfway to his mouth like he was about to say, "My boy, I'm going to tell you."

But he never said a word.

At night, I made the rounds twice. When a light moved far out on the sea, I pretended a boat was out there, but I knew it was only the beam from the lighthouse, and there's nothing else in the whole world and in life: only the ocean with a lighthouse stuck on a rock, some rabbits, some white birds, and us, and, every Wednesday, a boat that comes up out of the sea and then sinks back into it, comes up again the next week, then sinks, over and over.

I went back inside to bed. My father was looking at the window where you couldn't see a thing. I went to sleep, and, in my night, I saw flowers on green bushes that weren't moving, and no sound from the waves. The bushes were planted in black earth and everything was green and red and black, and in my night I never touched them, not the red flowers or the leaves like bird wings, only still. And I was there, too, beside it, lying down with my eyes pressed into the black earth.

Everything everywhere was quiet until a hand and a voice on my head. I opened my eyes, my father had pulled up a chair, and was beside me, watching me. He was going to tell me what was important, the big thing that had been waiting since morning. I waited. He told me they were closing the lighthouse on New Year's and that we would be leaving before that.

Leaving. What did it mean? Disappearing like my brother or sinking below the horizon like the man from the Coast Guard and his boat? I didn't want to hear this leaving. I wanted to go back again to the red flowers and my eyes in the soft black earth.

My father told me what the representative said that morning. No more boats came by here anymore. The lighthouse was finished. They would put out the big lantern. What about an accident with a boat that was lost? They would make arrangements of some kind, an unmanned light, no people on the island anymore. I was listening but didn't want to listen, I wanted to go back to my night.

My father was trying to convince me by talking like the representative. I half expected that screechy laugh. I was alone already almost. My father was a representative, and I was the only employee of lighthouses and buoys, and I left my red flowers behind to watch my brother - how he'll come back and see no one, he'll climb up, round and round the stairs to the lantern to call us, he'll see nothing but rust and salt where the light used to be, and the railing hanging in the wind. I could see him look everywhere, but my father was going on and on worse than the representative. There was work for him on the mainland, a factory where they would use him to make canned food or to put fish inside the cans.

He wanted to know how they close the cans and keep the air out of them. He said they must do it really fast, like when the downstairs door slams shut in a storm. He was saying he wasn't worried about not knowing how to do it, 'cause they would teach him. He never sounded like that before, his voice was all screechy like the representative, like someone who spends his whole life closing fish cans really fast.

I said that I would stay here on the island for when my brother comes back. My father's voice stopped, and I went to sleep again.

Next day, my father went back to his silence.

That night, the same story, wanting to say something he didn't. I went to sleep. The flowers and bushes were all gone, only black and no earth. And my father woke me up in the middle of the night, right there beside me. Quiet again, for awhile, then he begins the worst.

He says that I will leave with him Wednesday.

I told him no, what about my brother, he can't come back and find no one.

Then my father begins the worst, worse than all the leavings.

His chair right beside me, his voice cold like the downstairs door blown open.

He says that I didn't have a brother, that I never had one.

My brother was only me wanting to have one, to fill up the boredom. That's what he said, he said I never had a brother. He said it like he was crying, and he had another voice now, and it sounded really true and it scared me.

He said I played both parts, that I made up my brother and he became real. I learned to read believing the voice of the story was my brother, and my father had let this brother live in my head so I wouldn't be alone.

He asked me if I knew my brother's name. I didn't answer him.

He said that he had done everything to protect this wanting my brother, but I was the one who took the books, it was me who grabbed them like little sugars, and I was the only employee of lighthouses and buoys when he went out to look at his snares. I took my brother and his stories from those books.

I didn't believe it. And I cried with my father. He said that he was the one who killed my brother inside my head, by telling the man from the Coast Guard to stop bringing books because I was big and the stories were finished, the stories were finished.

Finished. That was the worst for me, worse than the horizon that disappears when it gets mixed up in the sky and the sea, worse than the dog dying. The dog, he existed. My brother, never.

My father told me that I had to know the truth, so I wouldn't be waiting anymore, so I would wait for life, for other people, not for my make-believe brother.

"But the mountains? The windmills? The towns?"

All from books, said my father, nothing from my brother's mouth or anyone else's. They were from books, and I knew how to read if I really wanted to, because I could make my brother talk without getting lost in the words or their pictures. The proof was that I could speak. He said that I knew how to leave each word and go on to the next ones. And his name. The proof was that I didn't know my brother's name or what he looked like.

I was crying, and banging my head on the soft mattress.

My father was going on and on with his proofs. But that didn't prove anything - his face or his name - because I remember my brother. I remember him - the proofs were all wrong. And then, suddenly, my head fell down into the mattress and I found my night again, and the earth. But I was looking inside the earth, there was no red or green spots, no flowers or bushes. Just the earth all by itself. And I went to sleep.

That was Thursday, and I was sick.

For the next few days, my father was busy filling up old crates with things I could see when I opened my eyes, then I closed them again, really fast.

I woke up on Wednesday, the day we had to leave, the last day of the month, the year, the last day of the lighthouse, this morning.

My father was still asleep. Everything was night. I left the downstairs and went outside. I was all better now. I went to the top of the cliff. I left my shoes at the foot of the cross, like I was going to jump. Then I went back down by the cove and up into the hole in the cliff where I used to play with my brother. After the sun came up, I never moved.

In a while, I saw my father running along the beach, shouting, banging against the rocks. I was all curled up in a ball, hiding.

My father must have gone all over the island looking for me like he did for my brother, only not pretending this time. The Coast Guard boat arrived, with the man and someone else.

My father went back down to the cove. I didn't know him because of the sweat, because of the tears all over his face. He was saying no again with his head. He must have told the man from the Coast Guard that I was gone. They looked at the bottom of the cliff and my father climbed back up to the lighthouse. The man from the Coast Guard stayed on the rocks below me.

He said to the other man, "Hopeless case." Then he said, "Poor guy, his son wasn't too bright." And he tapped his finger on his head. The other one said, "He only had one?" The man from the Coast Guard put his head down, and I couldn't hear anymore. Only, later, when the other one said, "And your little one?" And the man from the Coast Guard said, "Tonight, it's tonight. She's having it tonight."

He was looking at the island and smiling. He never wanted to see it again, or the lighthouse, just like my father who came back with the sadness that changed his face. They made him get into the boat, and he sat down on the bottom at the back, and closed his eyes.

When he opened them again, he was looking right at me, but lower down, below the cliff, where it's dangerous because the waves smash on the rocks and go round and round.

He thought I was in the holes at the bottom of the sea, but I was inside the cliff watching him.

The big mark of the boat and the three men moved slowly off the pebble beach towards the first breakers, that let them go by. And then the island slipped slowly away from the boat, the island where I was, slipped away like the rabbit swimming towards the open sea. And I was all curled up, like a periwinkle, cold and frozen.

I left with the cliff and the lighthouse, far from the boat, from my father. From the man from the Coast Guard and his little one who would come that night, who would be born from the girl with the red cloth.

That was this morning, number thirty-one on the calendar.

The light is still there, it's lost to the rest of the earth. I open my eyes, I close them. Who says we only see what's true when they're open? Up above, the big lantern is still turning. Midnight soon, the last ride at the fair. My brother used to talk about that, those rides going round and round like windmills.

I'm waiting for my brother. He will be happy to see the employee of lighthouses and buoys, me, waiting for him until the last turning of the lighthouse. Midnight, soon. The girl with the red cloth must have her baby now. But if my brother doesn't exist, why does this girl? Her baby who is coming? The man from the Coast Guard? And my father? Nothing knows if he exists.

And me?

Nothing goes out with the last turn from the lighthouse. What's true is when you close your eyes, the darkness lights up and turns.

It's my ride. It's my windmill. It still turns. It's turning.

Black.

About the playwright:

Timothée de Fombelle was born in 1973. He lives in Paris.
His play *Le Phare* was first produced in September 2001 at the
Théâtre du Marais (Paris) and won the Prix du Souffleur in 2002.
Je danse toujours was presented in the official line-up of the
prestigious Festival d'Avignon/2002 and was published by Éditions
Actes Sud in 2003. *Rose Cats* and *Saint Pierre sous terre*, both
comedies, were produced in Paris in 2004 and 2005, respectively.
Timothée de Fombelle also writes for the radio (*La mouche du
Pharaon*, France Culture 2003; *Je sais tout*, France Culture 2006).
He is currently working on two new plays, *Vango* and *Jazz Boxe*. His
first novel *Tobie Lolness* was published in 2006 by Gallimard-
Jeunesse.

About the translator:

Don Hannah is a playwright, novelist and director.
Shoreline, a collection of his plays, is published by Simon and Pierre,
and his novel *The Wise and Foolish Virgins*, is published by Knopf
Canada, who will also be publishing his second novel, *Ragged
Islands*, in 2007. *Facing South*, his opera with composer Linda C.
Smith, premiered at the 2003 World Stage Festival. He is founding
member of the Playwrights Atlantic Resource Centre and, for the
last eight years, has directed the Tarragon Theatre's Young
Playwrights Unit. He has been writer-in-residence at the Tarragon
and Canadian Stage theatres, the University of New Brunswick, the
Yukon Library, and was recently named the Lee Playwright in
Residence at the University of Alberta.

Don Hannah thanks Linda Gaboriau, Maureen Labonté, and John Murrell
for their affection and support. He would also like to acknowledge the lay
of the land at West Head, Nova Scotia, and the importance of every walk
taken at that wild and beautiful place.